Surface™ FOR DUMMIES®

by Andy Rathbone

WILEY

John Wiley & Sons, Inc.

Surface™ For Dummies®

Published by
John Wiley & Sons, Inc.
111 River Street
Hoboken, NJ 07030-5774

www.wiley.com

Copyright © 2013 by John Wiley & Sons, Inc., Hoboken, New Jersey

Published by John Wiley & Sons, Inc., Hoboken, New Jersey

Published simultaneously in Canada

For general information on our other products and services, please contact our Customer Care Department within the U.S. at 877-762-2974, outside the U.S. at 317-572-3993, or fax 317-572-4002.

For technical support, please visit www.wiley.com/techsupport.

Wiley publishes in a variety of print and electronic formats and by print-on-demand. Some material included with standard print versions of this book may not be included in e-books or in print-on-demand. If this book refers to media such as a CD or DVD that is not included in the version you purchased, you may download this material at http://booksupport.wiley.com. For more information about Wiley products, visit www.wiley.com.

Library of Congress Control Number: 2012955841

ISBN 978-1-118-49634-3 (pbk); ISBN 978-1-118-53462-5 (ebk); ISBN 978-1-118-49666-4 (ebk); ISBN 978-1-118-49657-2 (ebk)

Manufactured in the United States of America

10 9 8 7 6 5 4 3 2

WILEY

About the Author

Andy Rathbone started geeking around with computers in 1985 when he bought a 26-pound portable CP/M Kaypro 2X. Like other nerds of the day, he soon began playing with null-modem adapters, dialing computer bulletin boards, and working at Radio Shack.

He wrote for various techie publications before moving to computer books in 1992. He's written the *Windows For Dummies* series, *Upgrading and Fixing PCs For Dummies*, *Windows 8 For Tablets For Dummies*, and many other computer books.

Today, he has more than 15 million copies of his books in print, and they've been translated into more than 30 languages. You can reach Andy at his website, www.andyrathbone.com, where he answers a reader's question online each week.

Author's Acknowledgments

Special thanks to Dan Gookin, Matt Wagner, Tina Rathbone, Katie Mohr, Linda Morris, Matthew Baxter-Reynolds, and Wordsmith Editorial.

Thanks also to all the folks I never meet in editorial, sales, marketing, layout, and graphics who work hard to bring you this book.

Publisher's Acknowledgments

We're proud of this book; please send us your comments at http://dummies.custhelp.com. For other comments, please contact our Customer Care Department within the U.S. at 877-762-2974, outside the U.S. at 317-572-3993, or fax 317-572-4002.

Some of the people who helped bring this book to market include the following:

Acquisitions and Editorial

Project Editor: Linda Morris

Acquisitions Editor: Katie Mohr

Technical Editor: Matthew Baxter-Reynolds

Editorial Manager: Jodi Jensen

Editorial Assistant: Anne Sullivan

Sr. Editorial Assistant: Cherie Case

Cover Photo: Background © christina veit/ iStockphoto. Image of device and screenshot provided by author.

Cartoons: Rich Tennant (www.the5thwave.com/)

Composition Services

Project Coordinator: Patrick Redmond

Layout and Graphics: Ana Carrillo, Jennifer Creasey, Joyce Haughey

Proofreaders: John Greenough, Lauren Mandelbaum, Wordsmith Editorial

Indexer: BIM Indexing & Proofreading Services

Publishing and Editorial for Technology Dummies

Richard Swadley, Vice President and Executive Group Publisher

Andy Cummings, Vice President and Publisher

Mary Bednarek, Executive Acquisitions Director

Mary C. Corder, Editorial Director

Publishing for Consumer Dummies

Kathleen Nebenhaus, Vice President and Executive Publisher

Composition Services

Debbie Stailey, Director of Composition Services

Contents at a Glance

Table of Contents

Introduction

*W*elcome to *Surface For Dummies*! This book helps you wring the most out of your Surface: Microsoft's combination work/pleasure tablet that's turning heads on TV screens, coffee shops, classrooms, and lunch rooms.

This book doesn't explain everything you can do with the Surface. That would take at least ten volumes. No, this book explains everything you need to know to set up your Surface, introduce it to yourself and your social networks, and to transform it into a natural extension of your life.

About This Book

Today, most people think of a desktop PC as a workhorse for creating: They create documents, spreadsheets, and whatever other boring files their boss requires. And they usually require a mouse and keyboard.

Tablets, by contrast, work best at letting you consume: videos, music, the Internet, and e-mail. And it's often done on the couch, with your fingertips. But what if one tablet straddled both worlds, letting you both consume and create?

That's the promise of Microsoft's Surface tablet. Its finger-friendly Start screen lets you watch videos, listen to music, read e-books and e-mail, and browse the web. And, come Monday morning, you can switch to the Windows desktop, click on one of the Surface's two keyboards, and put on your working cap.

And how well does it hold up on that promise? That's where this book comes into play. I describe how it works in both work and play mode, and how to give it a few little tweaks to make it fit into your life a little more easily.

How to Use this Book

Instead of bundling a user manual with the Surface, Microsoft tossed in a single strip of paper with Ikea-like diagrams of how to fold down your Surface's kickstand. That's it.

This book takes over from that ignoble start by explaining exactly what you can and can't do with your Surface. And when it points out things you *can't* do, it offers some workarounds for going ahead and doing them anyway. The book comes separated into basic parts, each dealing with what you need to do with your Surface at certain times: Setting it up, connecting it to things, letting it entertain you, and buckling it down when work beckons.

Jump to the section you need at that particular moment in your life, absorb what you need to know, and move on. There's no need to read the entire thing from cover to cover. Everything's presented in easily digestible nuggets.

Everything presented here works with a tap of your Surface's touchscreen. On those rare occasions where you need to type information on a keyboard, you see easy-to-follow bold text like this: Type **Sarcophagus** into the Settings box. If you're reading this book as an e-book, you'll find all the websites are listed as *real* links, ready to direct you to the page with a tap of your finger.

Foolish Assumptions

Because you've purchased this book, I'm making one logical assumption about you: You've bought a Microsoft Surface tablet, or you're thinking about buying one.

So, you should know that everything in this book covers *both* models of Microsoft's Surface tablet:

- ✔ The Surface with Windows RT and Office Home & Student 2013 RT Preview, which I simply call "Surface with Windows RT" in this book.
- ✔ The Surface with Windows 8 Pro.

This book describes how the two models differ, and I place a special icon next to material that applies only to the Surface with Windows RT.

If you haven't yet purchased a Surface, this book helps you understand how the two models differ, and which model works best in which situations.

How This Book Is Organized

In Chapters 1–5, I explain why to consider buying a Surface, and which of the two models best meets your needs. I explain how to identify a Surface's buttons, ports, and sensors, how to attach its keyboard, and how to charge the battery.

Then I walk you through turning on the Surface for the first time, setting it up for your language, and downloading all of the waiting updates, including security updates and updates for its bundled apps and programs.

The beauty of the Surface comes from the way it can connect with so many different gadgets. Unlike other tablets, your Surface includes a built-in USB port and video port.

Chapters 6–9 walk you through connecting to the Internet, networked PCs, printers, portable accessories like flash drives, monitors, TVs, as well as projectors for giving presentations. I cover all of your available storage spaces, including flash drives, portable hard drives, networked PCs, and online spaces like SkyDrive. I also explain browsing and e-mail, as well as managing your social connections, making sure the Surface connects with Facebook, Twitter, LinkedIn, Flickr, and other networks.

A tablet wouldn't be any fun without leisure time, and Chapters 10 and 11 explain your Surface's built-in apps for viewing photos and movies, as well as listening to music, both your own and music purchased through Microsoft's Xbox music store.

Unlike other tablets, the Surface assumes you'll be doing some work, and Chapter 12 explains how the Windows desktops differ on the Windows RT and Windows 8 Pro versions. Chapter 13 covers the basics of Microsoft Word, Excel, PowerPoint, and OneNote. Those programs come built-in to the Surface RT and can be purchased at extra cost for the Surface Pro.

Because customizing and tweaking a computer's settings always involve work, I explain where to find each setting in Chapter 14 and which switches affect which behavior.

If you want more information about the desktop portion of your Surface, look for my book *Windows 8 For Dummies*, published by John Wiley & Sons, Inc. Written primarily for desktop computer owners, it covers tablets, but aims at helping mouse and keyboard owners make the most out of Windows 8.

A *For Dummies* tradition, Chapter 15 offers essential tips and tricks to get the most out of your Surface.

Icons Used in This Book

This book includes five basic *icons*, little symbols placed next to paragraphs of particular import. Here's what to expect when you see any of these icons:

Keep an eye out for this icon, which alerts you to time-saving tricks that immediately leapfrog you ahead of other Surface owners.

Avert your eyes from paragraphs marked with this icon — it contains archaic details that appeal to only a few nerdy souls.

Remember these few key tidbits, and you'll pick up things much more quickly.

Tread carefully with the steps in this paragraph. The information may cause serious damage to your files if things go wrong.

The Surface with Windows RT differs from the Surface with Windows 8 Pro in a few fundamental ways. This icon calls out information that explains those differences.

Where to Go from Here

New Surface owners should definitely start with a read-through of the first four chapters, with a special emphasis on Chapter 3. The walkthrough steps in there apply not only to you, but to everybody with their own account on your Surface.

If you don't have an attached keyboard, spend some time with Chapter 5; that chapter explains the subtleties of your Surface's built-in keyboard, which pops up when no other keyboard is attached.

Gadget hounds should jump to Chapters 6 through 9 to see exactly what will and won't work with the RT and Pro versions, as well as to set up their apps and social networks.

After that, jump to your choice: the Work (Chapters 12 through 14) or Play (Chapters 10 and 11) parts of the book.

If you're reading this as an e-book, use your reader's Bookmark and Search features to find what you want.

And with that, enjoy your Surface! It's a bold move by Microsoft that signals Windows' future, and you're at the forefront.

Chapter 1

Which Microsoft Surface Do You Need?

In This Chapter

▶ Choosing between a Microsoft Surface and other tablets

▶ Selecting the right Microsoft Surface

▶ Understanding the difference between the Windows RT and Windows 8 Pro versions

*M*any people stay tied to a desktop PC at work. They sit in front of a deskbound workhorse that lets them create files: documents, spreadsheets, and whatever other humdrum files their boss requires that day.

When it's time to relax, however, many of those same people reach for a tablet. Lightweight and portable, tablets make it easy to watch videos, listen to music, browse the web, and check e-mail.

But what if you had a tablet that did it *all?* You could *create* files when work called, but *consume* files during your leisure.

That's the promise of Microsoft's Surface tablet. Its finger-friendly Start screen lets you switch between videos, music, ebooks, e-mail, and the web. And, come Monday morning, you can switch to the Windows desktop, fire up Word, Excel, or PowerPoint, and get down to working.

Currently, Microsoft sells the Surface only at its retail locations and through its online store (www.microsoftstore.com).

This chapter explains Microsoft's two models of Surface tablets – the Surface with Windows RT and the Surface with Windows 8 Pro. I explain them both in detail, describing their features, their strengths, and their weaknesses.

Why Buy a Microsoft Surface?

Most computer manufacturers create Windows tablets as cheaply as possible. By coming up with the lowest price tag, they hope to undercut their competitors. Instead of taking this same road to the bottom, Microsoft created the Surface as a showpiece, designed to show off Windows 8 tablets at their finest.

To do that, Microsoft designed the Surface in-house with a large budget and engineering team, a luxury not available to most computer manufacturers.

Competitors cut costs by wrapping their tablets in cheap plastic. Microsoft's Surface, by contrast, comes sheathed in a magnesium alloy. This rugged but lightweight casing gives the Surface a solid feel.

The Surface includes a built-in kickstand, shown in Figure 1-1. An optional attachable keyboard doubles as a cover when not in use.

Why not just buy an iPad? Well, they're attractive tablets that excel at what they do, but they're limited. Without a USB port, you can't easily move files between an iPad and a desktop PC. Both Surface models, by contrast, include a USB port, making it easy to swap files through flash drives or even portable hard drives.

Figure 1-1: The Surface includes a kickstand to prop it up at a comfortable viewing angle.

And when iPad owners need to work, they usually reach for their laptop. Surface owners simply just flip their keyboard into place, load the familiar Windows desktop, and head for the mainstays of Microsoft Office: Word, PowerPoint, Excel, and OneNote.

When you're ready to hit the road again, flip back the keyboard and run, taking all of your files with you:

- Your Surface strips computing down to its essentials. Although it works without a keyboard, the optional keyboards add less than a half-pound of weight and doubles as a screen cover.

- When you plug a monitor into your tablet's video port, you've created a two-monitor workstation. You can view your notes on your tablet, but compose your document using the second, larger monitor. (I explain how to manage two monitors in Chapter 6.) Or, you can extend your Windows Desktop across both monitors, doubling its size.

- Touchscreens make many tasks much easier and faster. It's easy to scroll through large documents with a flick of your finger, for example. Plus, touchscreens often seem more natural, especially when paging through digital books, maneuvering through maps, or resizing digital photos.

Understanding the Unique Features of a Surface

Microsoft's Surface introduces several unique features not found in other tablets:

- **Kickstand:** Place a tablet on the desk, and its screen faces the ceiling, not you. To counter this, some tablets offer an expensive docking station that keeps your tablet at a convenient viewing angle. Although docks work well on a desk, they're difficult to carry around. To solve the problem, the Surface includes a built-in kickstand that lets your tablet sit upright like a laptop's screen.

- **Keyboard cover:** Most tablets don't include a case or a keyboard. You can buy them as accessories, but they're two more things to carry around. The Surface, by contrast, offers a keyboard that doubles as a cover. When you're done working, flip up the keyboard, and it becomes a cover to protect the screen.

- **USB port/memory card slot:** You'll find these on nearly every Windows tablet, but you won't find them on any iPad. Ask any iPad owner how they move information to and from their iPad. They all get an uncomfortable expression on their faces while explaining their workarounds.

✓ **Windows Desktop:** Nearly everybody has grown fairly used to the Windows Desktop, a staple around offices for two decades. Both the Surface with Windows RT and the Surface with Windows 8 Pro (more on the differences between those in the next section) include the Desktop, including Windows File Manager (formerly named Windows Explorer in Windows 7 and earlier versions of Windows). One caveat: You can't install traditional Desktop programs on the Surface with Windows RT.

✓ **Microsoft Office:** The RT version of Surface includes a copy of Office Home and Student 2013. That gives you Word, Excel, PowerPoint and OneNote, ready to create your own documents or touch up those that arrive in e-mail.

Deciding Between the Two Microsoft Surface Tablets

Microsoft sells two types of Surface tablets: Windows 8 Pro tablets, and Windows RT tablets. The two models look and behave almost identically. Both share many features:

✓ Windows 8 Pro's new tile-filled Start screen

✓ The Windows desktop

✓ Downloadable apps from the Windows store

✓ A USB port and memory card slot for adding storage

✓ The ability to create different accounts for different users

Yet the two tablets differ in subtle ways that lets them each serve different niches.

This section explains how the two models differ, letting you know whether Surface with Windows RT or Surface with Windows 8 Pro meets your needs.

Surface with Windows RT

No portable computer can compete with a desktop computer. Desktop computers don't need to be light, and they're permanently anchored to a wall outlet for power.

In order to stay lightweight and battery-powered, all laptops and tablets must make compromises.

The following section lists the good things about Surface with Windows RT; the next section lists the bad.

The Good

The simple, minimalist RT version doesn't run Windows 8 but a new operating system called *Windows RT*. The Windows RT version of the Surface offers quite a few advantages over the Windows 8 version:

- **Lower price:** The 32GB version of Surface with Windows RT costs $499; adding a keyboard cover adds $120, and the 64 GB RT version costs $699. Tablets running Windows 8, by contrast, start at around $900.

- **Longer battery life:** Perhaps the biggest attraction is that the Windows RT version runs for eight hours or more before needing a recharge. Plug its charger into the wall, and two hours later, you're ready to go. If you don't use it a lot, it can live without a recharge for several days.

- **Connected standby:** Even while it's asleep, the Windows RT version remains connected with the Internet, fetching your latest e-mail in the background. And as soon as you touch it, it wakes up, looking just like you left it.

- **USB support:** The Windows RT version works well with natively recognized USB gadgets. That means you can plug in storage devices (flash drives, portable drives), USB hubs with more USB ports, mice, keyboards, cameras, headsets, and some USB printers.

- **Bluetooth support:** Nearly anything that connects wirelessly through Bluetooth works well with Windows RT. Your wireless headsets, mice, keyboards, and other Bluetooth gadgets should work without a hitch.

- **Memory card slot:** To add storage, slide a memory card into the microSDHX slot. That slot works with microSD, microSDHC, or microSDHX cards, which let you add 64GB storage space. Higher-capacity cards are on their way.

- **Microsoft Office:** The RT version includes Microsoft Office Home and Student 2013 RT, which comes with Word, PowerPoint, Excel, and OneNote. That's one less thing to buy to stay productive.

- **Apps:** Surface RT runs apps downloaded from the Windows Store. The Store doesn't have as many apps as Apple and Google offer, but the stock grows larger every day.

Surface with Windows RT works best during your leisure time, letting you watch movies, listen to music, browse the web, and connect with your friends.

Should you need to work, open the Desktop app. There, the built-in Microsoft Word, Excel, PowerPoint, and OneNote apps should carry you through until you can get back to the office.

The Bad

In order to meet its exceptional battery life, the Surface RT brings some unique compromises. Some will be deal breakers. Other people will say, "Who needs that, anyway?"

Here they are, in no particular order:

- **No desktop programs:** Surface RT can only run apps downloaded from the App store. You can't install desktop programs, like you can on a desktop PC.

- **No Windows Media Center:** Unlike Windows 8 computers, Surface RT won't let you install Windows Media Center for watching or recording TV shows.

- **No Windows Media Player:** Windows RT's Desktop doesn't include Windows Media Player. To watch movies and listen to music, you must use the Surface RT's built in Music and Video apps, or download new apps from the Windows Store.

- **Can't start a homegroup:** When connected to a network, the Surface RT can join homegroups and access files from other networked computers. However, those computers can't access *your* files. To share your files, you can either upload them to SkyDrive, copy them to a portable flash drive (or hard drive), or send them through e-mail.

- **No driver support:** Windows RT requires its own set of *drivers* — special software that lets it communicate with plugged-in accessories. Without drivers, it won't work with some USB gadgets like network adapters, TV tuners, barcode readers, GPS units, and other devices. (Windows 8 drivers won't work; the drivers must be written specifically for Windows RT.)

- **No GPS:** Lacking a GPS chip, the Surface with Windows RT relies on Wi-Fi to estimate your location. That narrows down your location to within a few hundred feet.

- **No NFC (Near Field Communication):** Too new of a technology to disappoint many, NFC lets two devices exchange bursts of information when they bump into each other, like shoppers in a crowded grocery aisle.

> ✔ **Limited storage space:** A 32GB Surface RT only leaves you with 20GB of storage space. The operating system consumes a whopping 12GB.

The Windows RT version of Surface differs from the Windows 8 Pro version in many subtle ways too numerous to mention here. If you own a Surface RT, keep an eye open for this Windows RT icon, like the one in the margin. Paragraphs with this icon explain other ways your Surface RT differs from the Surface with Windows 8 Pro.

Surface with Windows 8 Pro

Whereas the Surface with Windows RT aims to meet the consumer's needs, the Surface with Windows 8 Pro gives professionals all the power of a desktop PC in a rugged tablet. You could say that it's two computers in one. On one hand, you have the Start screen apps for casual, on-the-go computing and staying connected while traveling.

And, when work calls, you can load the full-powered Windows 8 Desktop to run the same Windows programs you run on your desktop PC.

Windows 8 Pro also lets you pony up an extra $15 for the Windows Media Center Pack. This lets you play DVDs, if you plug in a USB DVD drive. Plug in a TV tuner, connect an TV signal from cable or an antenna, and you've turned the Surface into a complete digital video recorder, ready to record TV shows for watching later.

I won't list all the advantages here because the Surface with Windows 8 Pro is basically a desktop PC flattened into a tablet. *Any* software that runs on a Windows 8 desktop PC runs on a Surface Pro.

The same holds true for gadgets you plug into the Windows 8 Pro's USB port: network ports, bar code readers, scanners, MIDI gadgets, and other specialty items.

But all that power brings a few compromises:

> ✔ **Battery life:** The battery life is estimated at five hours.
>
> ✔ **No Microsoft Office:** Unlike the Windows RT version, the Windows 8 Pro version doesn't come with Microsoft Office. You need to buy and install it separately.
>
> ✔ **No connected standby:** When the tablet's asleep, it's *really* asleep. It won't collect your e-mail in the background.

Although the battery life might seem low, it might not be a limiting factor for you. Most people work at a desk with a nearby power outlet. That lets you plug in your Surface and keep on working.

Summing Up the Differences Between the Versions

Sometimes numbers mean more than words. To satisfy the other side of your brain, the specifications in Tablet 1-1 show exactly how the Surface RT and Surface Pro differ.

Table 1-1   Differences Between the Windows RT and Windows 8 Pro Versions

Item	Windows RT	Windows 8 Pro
Processor	Quad-core NVIDIA Tegra 3	Third-generation Intel Core i5 Processor with Intel HD Graphics 4000
Memory	2GB	4GB
Weight	1.5 pounds	2 pounds
Thickness	.37 inches (9.3mm)	.53 inches (13.5mm)
Display	10.6 inches, 16:9 ratio, 1366×763 pixels, 5 point multitouch	10.6 inches, 16:9 ratio, 1920×1080 pixels, 10-point multitouch
Battery	31.5 watt hours	42 watt hours
Ports	USB 2.0 slot, micro-HDMI port, microSDHX slot, 1/8 inch head-phone jack, stereo speakers	USB 3.0 slot, mini-Display Port, microSDHX slot, 1/8 inch headphone jack, stereo speakers
Wireless	Wi-Fi (802.11a/b/g/n), Bluetooth 4.0	Wi-Fi (802.11a/b/g/n), Bluetooth 4.0
Storage capacity	32GB or 64GB	64GB or 128GB

Item	Windows RT	Windows 8 Pro
Cameras	Two 720p cameras, front and rear	Two 720p cameras, front and rear
Price	$499 for 32GB, $599 for 32GB and Touch cover; $699 for 64GB and Touch cover	$899 for 64GB, $999 for 128GB; Touch covers sold separately
Start screen	Yes	Yes
Office (Word, Excel, PowerPoint, OneNote)	Yes, includes Home and Student version	No. Office must be purchased and installed separately
Stylus	Not included, but supports capacitive stylus	Digital stylus included, with built-in charger
Sensors	Ambient light sensor, accelerometer, gyroscope, compass	Ambient light sensor, accelerometer, gyroscope, compass
Power supply	24 watts (included)	48 watts, with 5-watt USB port for charging accessories

Upgrading to Windows 8.1

One year after the release of Windows 8, Microsoft released Windows 8.1. Shortly afterward, Microsoft released two new models of its Surface tablet:

- **Surface 2:** Just as with its predecessor, the Surface RT, the Surface 2 only runs *apps* downloaded from the Windows Store; you can't install desktop programs. However, the Surface 2 comes with two desktop programs preinstalled: Office 2013 RT, which is basically Office 2013 Home and Student version, and Outlook RT, an e-mail program.

- **Surface Pro 2:** Similar to the Surface Pro described in this book, the Surface Pro 2 can run any Windows program, much like a desktop computer.

The new Surface models run either Windows 8.1 or Windows 8.1 RT, and they're both thinner, lighter, and faster than their predecessors.

Windows 8 owners — including current Surface owners — may upgrade without charge to Windows 8.1. Owners of Windows 7 or older operating systems must pay for the upgrade.

Windows 8.1 changes Windows 8 quite a bit, and mostly for the better. You'll find the upgrade waiting for you in the Windows Store. (If you don't spot it on the opening page, find it by searching for *Windows 8.1* in the Search box.)

After installing Windows 8.1, desktop lovers can boot straight to the desktop, skipping the Start screen completely. Accordingly, Start screen lovers can prolong their stay on the Start screen, as its settings area now includes many features formerly limited to the desktop.

Windows 8.1 also embeds SkyDrive, Microsoft's cloud storage space, directly into Windows. Formerly available from either a web browser or installable program, SkyDrive now appears in every folder in Windows 8.1. By storing your most important files on SkyDrive, you can read and update them from any computer, tablet, or phone. When you update your SkyDrive files from one device, those updated files are quickly available to *all* of your other devices. Windows 8.1 includes seven gigabytes of free online storage space.

Windows 8.1 offers other perks, including the return of the Start button to the desktop. Its App store now holds more than 125,000 apps, including an official Facebook app. Windows 8.1 shaves off Windows 8's rough edges, making it much less cumbersome to use.

If you don't like change, or you don't want this book's instructions to go out of date, you should stick with Windows 8. But if you're upgrading to Windows 8.1 or buying a new Surface model, check out this book's second edition.

In the meantime, you'll find free online information and tutorials about Windows 8.1 at `dummies.com/extras/windows8dot1fd`.

Chapter 2

Getting Started with Your Surface

*W*hether your Surface arrives in the mail or in a shopping bag from your local Microsoft Store, the fun doesn't start right away. No, first you need to remove Surface from the packaging (easy) and charge the battery (challenging) — tasks I cover in this chapter.

While you're waiting for the battery to charge, take some time to identify all of your Surface's ports, slots, and attachments, all described in this chapter. Some of them sit in plain sight; others hide in mysterious crevices.

But no matter where they hide, this chapter points them all out so you know what each one does. That way, you can either impress your friends or bore them to tears with your Surface port acumen.

The Grand Unboxing

The Surface comes artfully packed in black box, shown in Figure 2-1. Look closely at the top-right corner, and you can see a white box protruding from inside. It's either an artful display of design creativeness or a waste of paper, depending on your mood.

Figure 2-1: The Surface comes packaged in a white box that's been pushed inside a black box.

To unpack your Surface from its packaging, follow these steps:

1. **Remove the small strip of clear plastic tape holding the white box to the black sleeve.**

2. **Slide the white box out of the black sleeve.**

3. **Remove the touch keyboard and its black cardboard packaging from the beneath the box.**

   If you bought a Surface without a keyboard, you won't find the keyboard. (Unless the salesperson handed you the wrong box by mistake, in which case you're stuck with an ethical dilemma.)

4. **Push up the keyboard up and out of the thin cardboard packaging.**

   Push up the keyboard from below and it rises out of the box.

5. **Remove the keyboard's instructions from the secret hiding place inside the thin cardboard packaging.**

   The keyboard's instruction manual, shown in Figure 2-2, is one sheet of paper with pictures of how the keyboard attaches to the Surface. Spoiler: Magnets in both the Surface and the keyboard make them click together whenever they're an inch apart.

Figure 2-2: The keyboard's instructions hide in a crevice in the cardboard holder.

6. **Remove the small strip of plastic tape holding the white box shut, and then open the lid. (The lid opens, with the hinge along the right edge.)**

   As the lid opens, you see the Surface resting peacefully inside, shown in Figure 2-3, complete with its power adapter.

Figure 2-3: The Surface RT includes a power adapter, thankfully.

7. **Remove the Surface from the box and remove its plastic wrapper.**

8. **Remove the manual from the box beneath the Surface and remove the charger.**

And that's it. The Surface's battery comes partially charged, but before turning it on, you should probably plug it into the charger, described in the next section. When you're ready to turn on your Surface, flip ahead to Chapter 3.

⊯ The Surface's manual, like the manual for its keyboards, are simply illustrations with IKEA-inspired instructions: single sheets of paper with illustrations and arrows.

⊯ Your Surface's serial number is listed on the box (it's written above the middle bar of the three bar codes).

⊯ Your Surface's serial number and memory size also appears hidden underneath the Surface's kickstand.

⊯ The serial number for the keyboard appears on the right edge of its spine.

⊯ If your Surface needs to be returned for service, you need to enter the serial number on Microsoft's online support site.

⊯ Okay, if you can't wait, feel free to use the Surface while it's charging. But flip ahead to Chapter 4, where I walk you through the process.

Charging the Battery

The Surface's bundled charger is lightweight, smaller, and flatter than many adapters, making it easy to carry. In the North American version, the outlet's prongs make nice little clicks as they fold in and out, just like the keyboards do.

But although the charger plugs into the wall easily, politely leaving room to plug something into the adjacent outlet, the charger's other end isn't quite as well designed. Theoretically, its five little metal pins line up with the five little metal pins on your Surface's right edge.

Practically, though, the charger is difficult to attach, and it often leaves you wondering whether it's even charging your device. That's not a good feeling at the airport. You'll regain your confidence with this little secret:

When attached correctly, a little light begins glowing on the charger's flat end. If you don't see that little light, try wiggling the charger until it seats more firmly in the slot.

Follow these steps to charge your Microsoft Surface:

1. **Unfold the prongs from the charger's long end, if necessary, and plug them into an outlet.**

   On North American models, the prongs fold in for easy storage and out for plugging into a wall. Plug the charger into the wall so it doesn't cover the second wall outlet, and you'll leave room for plugging in other gadgets.

2. Place the prong's small end into the charger on your tablet's lower-right side.

The five magnetically charged metal ports on the end of the charger cable should mesh with the five magnetically charged ports on your tablet. The connector fits in either way, shown in Figure 2-4, with the cord pointing up or down your tablet's edge.

If the connector doesn't snap tightly into the groove, it won't charge – even when it *feels* like it's in place. The key is to look for the little light on the flat part of the connector (shown in Figure 2-5). Keep rocking the connector from side to side until the light glows. Then don't touch it!

3. Wait for the Surface to charge.

Figure 2-4: The symmetrical connector fits into the charger socket either way.

A dead Surface with Windows RT charges to about 50 percent in an hour; it fills completely in another hour. The Surface with Windows 8 Pro takes a little longer to charge.

✔ The Surface can be charged only with its bundled proprietary charger. At the time of this writing, Microsoft doesn't offer any chargers that plug into a car's cigarette lighter.

✔ You can't charge the Surface from another computer's USB port.

✔ You *can* charge your phone or other USB gadgetry from the USB port of both Surface models. If possible, though, plug your Surface into the wall first.

✔ The Surface with Windows 8 Pro's power adapter puts out 48 watts to charge its large battery. Its adapter also includes a USB port for charging accessories, a handy feature missing from the RT version's power adapter.

When the light glows, your Surface is charging.

Figure 2-5: When the connector's light glows, you've successfully fastened it, and the Surface begins charging.

Figuring Out What's Included and What's Missing

The only things included in the box are the Surface, its charger, and a thin sheet of paper. (That's your manual.)

Unless you paid extra for accessories, Microsoft left out these popular items, unfortunately:

✔ **Keyboard:** The Surface's Touch keyboard ($120) and Type keyboard ($130) can be purchased at Microsoft's online store (www.microsoftstore.com) or at any Microsoft store retail location. Designed specifically for the Surface, they also fold over the screen as a cover. I describe them both in more detail in Chapter 5.

   If you don't want to spring for the expensive Touch or Type covers, you can plug any desktop PC keyboard into the USB port. Bluetooth (wireless) keyboards also work well.

- **Cables:** You can plug your Surface into an external monitor or HDMI TV set for watching movies, gaming, or just fiddling around. Unfortunately, Microsoft didn't include the cables. For more information on cables, flip ahead to Chapter 6.

- **Memory card:** The Surface includes a memory card slot, but it's empty. Adding a memory card adds storage, as I describe in the next section.

- **Stylus:** You can draw on your Surface with a plastic pen called a *stylus*, but the Windows RT version doesn't include a stylus. (The Windows 8 Pro version does.)

Identifying the Parts of Your Surface Tablet

Waiting for your battery to charge can be pretty boring. So, while you're waiting for your new Surface to charge fully for the first time, spend some time examining its front, back, and edges, as shown in Figure 2-6.

This section explains the holes, switches, and oddly shaped doo-dads on your Surface, what they do, and what they won't do.

- **On/Off toggle switch:** Pressing this simple on/off toggle switch in the top-right corner doesn't really turn your tablet on or off. Instead, it puts your tablet to *sleep*: a low-power state where your tablet shuts down everything but the essentials. Then, when you tap the On/Off toggle again, the Surface wakes up nearly instantly, with all of your open apps and documents just the way you left them.

- **Stereo microphones:** This pair of microphones, spaced four inches apart along your Surface's top edge, records stereo sound when you shoot movies, or when recording through apps.

- **Speakers:** This pair of speakers lives near the top of your Surface's sides, providing surprisingly good stereo separation. The speakers aren't extraordinarily loud, however, which is great for neighboring hotel rooms, but not so good in a crowded room.

- **microHDMI port (Surface RT):** Microsoft's website called this port along the right edge an "HD video port." That led many people to buy the $40 video cable so they could connect their Surface to an external monitor. The good news is that it's a plain old microHDMI port, so you can use *any* microHDMI cable, which usually costs around five dollars.

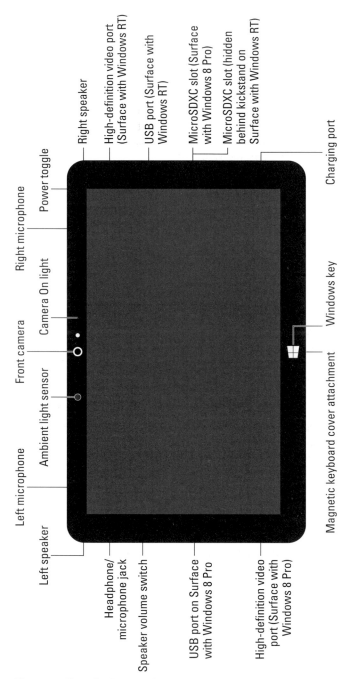

Right speaker

High-definition video port (Surface with Windows RT)

USB port (Surface with Windows RT)

MicroSDXC slot (Surface with Windows 8 Pro)

MicroSDXC slot (hidden behind kickstand on Surface with Windows RT)

Charging port

Power toggle

Right microphone

Camera On light

Front camera

Ambient light sensor

Left microphone

Left speaker

Windows key

Magnetic keyboard cover attachment

Headphone/ microphone jack

Speaker volume switch

USB port on Surface with Windows 8 Pro

High-definition video port (Surface with Windows 8 Pro)

Figure 2-6: Your Surface and its connectors.

- **miniDisplay Port (Surface Pro):** This newer type of port, often found Apple laptops, puts out higher resolution video through a miniDisplay Port cable.

- **USB port:** This port, the same size as the ones found on desktop PCs and laptops, lets you plug in keyboards, mice, portable hard drives, and other USB accessories. The RT version's USB port uses USB 2.0, while the Windows 8 Pro version includes USB 3.0, a newer, faster port. (Yes, you can charge your cell phone with this port, but plug in your Surface to avoid draining its battery.)

- **Charging port:** Described in the previous section, this odd five-button port on the lower-right side lets you charge your Surface with Microsoft's proprietary adapter.

- **Headphone jack:** Headphones and external speakers plug into this 1/8-inch port on the left side.

The headphone jack also accepts specially designed microphones. These microphones, compatible with iPhones and iPods, have three thin stripes on them and are slightly longer than regular microphones, which only have two thin stripes.

- **Volume control:** This rocker switch on the top-left side works as expected: Press the top portion to raise the volume; press the lower portion to lower it. As you press the control, the screen shows the current sound level. (You can also control the volume with a Touch or Type keyboard, covered in Chapter 5, or any keyboard with dedicated Windows 8 keys.)

- **Keyboard connector:** This mysterious magnetic connector on the bottom edge only works with the Touch or Type keyboards. To use standard keyboard, just plug the keyboard's USB plug into the USB port on your Surface's right edge. I describe how to connect Bluetooth keyboards, mice, and other accessories in Chapter 6.

- **Kickstand:** Folding flush against the Surface's lower back edge, this flips out to prop up your Surface when working at a desk. It works on laps, as well, but doesn't feel as substantial and flat as a traditional laptop. It opens easiest from either of the two bottom corners, and, in a boon for lefties, from the indent along the bottom-left side.

- **microSDHX slot.** Flip open the kickstand on the Surface with Windows RT and you'll spot the hidden microSDHX slot. The slot accepts a microSD, microSDHC, *or* a microSDHX card, the same type found in many cell phones for the past few years. (The same slot lives on the left edge of the Surface with Windows 8 Pro.) Many stores sell 64GB SDHX cards, with higher-capacity cards arriving soon.

✔ **Camera:** These two cameras, located on the top center of the Surface's front and back sides, only capture one-megapixel images; most cell phones capture at least five. But who takes photos with a tablet, anyway? One cool thing: The back camera is angled downward at 22 degrees, so it shoots straight when the tablet sits with its kickstand out on the table.

✔ **Recording light:** Barely visible next to each camera lens, this tiny white light glows whenever you're framing or shooting a photo a video. In fact, if you see it glowing, *smile*: you're being recorded.

✔ **Ambient light sensor:** Located just to the left of the front camera, this barely visible sensor constantly measures the light surrounding the screen. When you walk into a dark room, the screen dims slightly, making it easier to read (and preserving battery life). Similarly, walk outdoors in the sunlight, and the screen brightens to make it easier to read. I explain how to adjust it in Chapter 14 by visiting the PC Settings' General area and flipping a toggle in the Screen section.

✔ **Windows key button:** Located on the bottom front of your tablet, this looks more like a logo than a button. And it doesn't physically move when pressed. But your tablet senses your finger's presence and behaves as if you've pressed your keyboard's Windows key. It returns you to the Start screen. Or, if you're already at the Start screen, it returns you to your last-used program.

Attaching the Keyboard

The Surface's special Touch and Type keyboard covers adhere to the Surface by strong magnets, and they're not difficult to attach. Hold the keyboard's connector anywhere close to the connector on the Surface's bottom edge, shown in Figure 2-7, and they lunge for each other.

However, like tired wrestlers, they occasionally miss. (To test the connection, press the keyboard's Windows key; it should toggle the Surface between your Start menu and your last-used application.)

If your Surface doesn't acknowledge your keyboard's keystrokes, try holding down the keyboard and sliding the Surface to the left and right until you feel the keyboard lock into place.

Still not working? Try restarting your Surface with the keyboard attached: Swipe in from the screen's right edge to fetch the Charms bar, tap the Settings icon, tap the Power icon from the Settings pane, and tap Restart from the pop-up menu.

Figure 2-7: Match the Touch or Type keyboard's connector with the connector on the bottom of your Surface, and they click into place.

Still not working? Try wiping any oil or dirt from the two connectors. If it still doesn't work, it's time to drop by a Microsoft store in your city or contact Microsoft's Service Online Service Center (https://myservice.surface.com).

Positioning the Surface

Your Surface works in a variety of positions. First, it's a tablet. No matter how you hold it, the screen flips to be right-side up. Although convenient, it's also disorienting: The familiar power button on the top right suddenly lives on your bottom left.

To remember which side is *really up*, take a look at the white Windows logo button on the Surface's bottom front edge. When the logo's on the bottom, your tablet is right-side up, and all the buttons are where they should be. If it's on the top, juggle your button memory accordingly to match.

When you're seated, fold out the Surface's kickstand from the Surface's back: Place your finger in the indentation on the back's lower-left edge and pull out; the kickstand snaps into place.

Although it looks precarious, the Surface and its kickstand actually feel pretty solid on a lap.

Finding Microsoft Website Support for the Surface

Microsoft offers several official sites dealing with the Surface, its sales, and support:

- ✔ **Microsoft's Surface** (www.microsoft.com/surface): Microsoft's catch-all page for the Surface, this describes the two models in detail, lets you sign up for the mailing list for product announcements, and provides links to the online store and support pages.

- ✔ **Microsoft's Surface Support** (www.microsoft.com/surface/support): Visit here if your Surface doesn't seem to work correctly. You can walk through some troubleshooting steps, and if they don't work, you can contact Microsoft's technical support. They'll assess the situation, and then make arrangements for a replacement if it's still under warranty.

- ✔ **Windows 8 Compatibility Center** (www.microsoft.com/en-us/windows/compatibility): Here you can see what devices people report to have worked with Windows RT. Unfortunately, Microsoft tends to think everything is compatible until proven otherwise. Don't be surprised to see your incompatible items listed here as compatible.

Chapter 3

Setting Up Your Surface

. . . .

. . . .

*Y*ou've taken your Surface out of the box. You've charged the battery. You've attached the keyboard.

But your Surface *still* isn't ready for action.

This chapter walks you through everything you need to do when first turning on your Surface: Sign in with a Microsoft account (or create a new one), name your Surface, download updates, and then set up user accounts for everybody who will be using your Surface.

And, if you own a Surface with Windows RT, I explain how to upgrade your preview copy of Microsoft Office to the real deal.

Turning On Your Surface for the First Time

After prying off all the cardboard, peeling off the plastic wrappers, and charging your Surface, the fun begins. Follow these steps to turn on your Surface for the first time:

1. Press and release the power button on your Surface's top-right edge.

I describe all of your Surface's buttons in Chapter 2. Two or three seconds after you press and release the button, the word *Surface* appears in white letters on a black screen as your tablet churns its way to life. After a minute or two, it leaves you staring silently at the opening screen called *Your Display Language.*

If you made a mistake while following any of the next steps, hold down the Surface's power button for about five seconds until it turns off. Release the power button, wait a second, and then press and release it again to turn on your Surface. When your Surface wakes up, it begins at the opening step, letting you start over.

2. **Tap your favorite language from the list and tap Next.**

   As soon as you tap one of the listed languages, the Next button's wording changes to that language, giving you a visual warning that you're switching away from the tablet's startup language, English.

The screen goes blank when it's left untouched for more than one minute. To revive it, touch the Windows key centered beneath your screen. (Or, if you have a keyboard cover attached, tap any key.)

If you want to change your Surface's keyboard's layout to accommodate other languages, I explain how in Chapter 14.

3. **When the License Terms page appears, read the License Terms agreement, tap the I Accept the License Terms for Using Windows box, and tap the Accept button.**

   Pull up a chair and relax. The Surface RT agreement is almost 6,000 words long. (The Privacy agreement, available a few screens down the road, is more than 20,000 words.)

4. **When the Personalize screen appears, choose your Start screen's background color, type a name for your Surface into the PC Name box, and tap Next.**

   As you tap in different places on the colored strip shown in Figure 3-1, the background color changes to match the color beneath your finger. Spot a color you like? Lift your finger to lock that color into place. (I explain how to change the color in Chapter 14.)

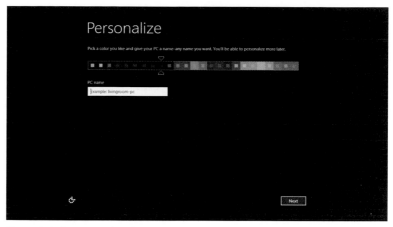

Figure 3-1: Slide your finger along the bar to choose a color and then create a name for your new Surface.

Next, tap in the PC Name box and type a name for your Surface. If you haven't attached a keyboard to your Surface, the tablet's built-in keyboard pop's up, letting you type in your Surface's new name. (I describe how to type on the built-in glass keyboard in Chapter 5.)

After choosing a color and name for your Surface, tap the Next button. (I explain how to change your Surface's tablet's name in Chapter 14.)

After you leave this screen, the subsequent screens all have a backward-pointing arrow in their top-left corner. Tapping a backward-pointing arrow lets you return to the previous screen and change any of your answers.

5. **When the Wireless screen appears, connect to a wireless network, if available, and tap Connect.**

   If you're within range of a wireless network, the Surface lists all the wireless networks it detects, shown in Figure 3-2. If you spot yours, tap its name and tap the Connect button. Type in your password, if required, and then tap Connect.

Figure 3-2: Tap a wireless network's name, and tap the Connect button to connect with the Internet.

Not within range? Don't know the password? Then tap the Connect to a Wireless Network Later link. I explain how to connect to wireless networks in Chapter 6.

6. **When the Settings screen appears, tap the Use Express Settings button.**

   The Express settings, shown in Figure 3-3, provide a good mix of security while preserving your privacy. If you prefer to personalize your settings, however, tap the Customize button. (I explain how to change these settings later in Chapter 14.)

Figure 3-3: Tap Use Express Settings to stick with Microsoft's selected settings, or tap Customize to approve each setting manually.

7. If you successfully connected with the Internet in Step 5, type in your e-mail address. If you didn't connect, create a Local account and then type in a name and password.

At this point, your path moves in different directions depending on whether you were able to connect with the Internet in Step 5.

- If you connected with the Internet and already have a Microsoft account — an e-mail address you use to visit Microsoft services like Hotmail, Messenger, SkyDrive, Windows Phone, Xbox LIVE, or Outlook.com — type that address into the white box and tap the Next button, shown in Figure 3-4. Enter your password at the next screen, tap Next, and move to the next steps to verify your security information.

- If you connected with the Internet but don't have a Microsoft account, type your favorite e-mail address into the white box. The setup program then walks you through the necessary steps to transform that e-mail address into a Microsoft account. (You need a Microsoft account to get the most out of your Surface tablet.)

- Couldn't connect with the Internet? Then create a Local account by typing your first name and a password. Then tap Finish.

No matter which path you take in Step 7, you end up staring at the Windows 8 Start screen. Welcome!

Figure 3-4: Type in your Microsoft account e-mail address, click Next, and type in your password.

Trusting your PC

Whenever you create a Microsoft account on a new Windows 8 PC — and your Surface counts as a PC — Microsoft asks you to "Trust This PC." The words *Trust This PC* may appear on a menu on your Surface or in an e-mail.

Trust it with what, you may ask? Actually, Microsoft wants to know if you trust this PC with your information. This security precaution ensures that *you're* the one accessing the PC. Here's how it works:

To verify your identity, Microsoft sends a secret code to the cell phone or e-mail address that you entered when first setting up your Microsoft account. When you receive the code, visit the listed web address and enter the code into the online confirmation box.

Microsoft then confirms that *you* are the person creating an account on the Surface, and it begins syncing all your passwords and sign-in information for your apps, websites, networks, and your network's homegroup, if you have one.

✔ If you signed in with a Microsoft account that you've owned for awhile, your Surface begins stocking itself with all of your settings. If you've kept any online contacts or appointments using that e-mail address, Windows 8 automatically stocks your contacts list and appointments, too.

✔ If you couldn't connect with the Internet and created a Local account, I explain how to turn a Local account into a much more convenient Microsoft account in this chapter's "Setting Up User Accounts" section.

Downloading Updates

No doubt, your new Surface has updates waiting for it. Some updates fix the latest bugs; others add features. Perhaps the most important update for Surface RT transforms the *preview* version of Office into the finished version.

Unfortunately, you need to run through two different hoops to grab all your updates. And, if you ever Reset or Refresh your Surface — Chapter 14's emergency efforts that revive a very sick Surface — you need to repeat them yet again.

To bring your Surface up to date with all the waiting updates, follow the steps in the next two sections.

Downloading updates from Windows Update

To download any waiting updates from Windows Update, follow these steps:

1. **Summon the Charms bar and tap the Settings icon.**

   Slide your finger in slightly from the screen's right edge to fetch the Charms bar, and then tap the Settings icon at the bar's bottom edge. The Settings pane appears.

2. **Tap the Change PC Settings link from the bottom of the Settings pane.**

   The PC Settings screen appears.

3. **Tap Windows Update from the screen's bottom-left corner and tap the We'll Install Important Updates Automatically link.**

   If Windows Update doesn't list any waiting updates, tap the link Check for Updates Now.

   Then, when Windows Update finds updates waiting, tap the We'll Install Important Updates Automatically link to see the list of waiting updates. That list, shown in Figure 3-5, doesn't list *optional* updates, though.

   Microsoft considers the finished version of Office 2013 RT to be an option. So, move ahead to Step 4.

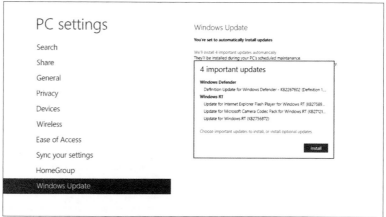

Figure 3-5: From the pop-up box, tap Choose Important Updates to Install or Install Optional Updates.

4. **Tap the words Choose Important Updates to Install or Install Optional Updates.**

   The Control Panel appears, opened on the traditional Windows Desktop.

5. **Tap the words Important Updates are Available.**

   Those words appear just beneath the words You're Set to Automatically Install Updates.

6. **When the Select Updates to Install window appears, select the Update for Office Home & Student Office Preview and then tap Install.**

   Tap the check mark next to the Update for Microsoft Office Home & Student 2013 RT Preview to select it.

7. **Tap the Install button.**

   The update for Microsoft Home and Office is huge and could take 10 to 30 minutes to complete, depending on your connection speed.

8. **Restart your Surface.**

   After you've downloaded all of the waiting updates, restart your Surface. If you're still looking at the Windows Update screen, tap the Restart Now button. If you're at any other screen, follow this step to restart your Surface:

   Summon the Charms bar by sliding your finger in from the screen's right edge, and then tap the Settings icon. Tap the Power button on the Settings pane, and when the pop-up menu appears, tap the words Update and Restart.

When your Surface returns to life, the updates are installed and your Surface is up to date. Now, you need to bring your *apps* up to date, as well, as described in the next section.

Downloading app updates from the Windows Store

Windows Update updates your *operating system* — Windows 8 or Windows RT. It doesn't update your *apps*, though. Those updates arrive automatically through the Store app. You can tell when the Store app contains waiting updates by looking at the Start screen: The Store app's green tile bears a number listing the number of waiting updates.

Creating a Recovery Drive

To be on the safe side, create a Recovery Drive for your Surface with Windows RT. Stored on a flash drive of 4GB or more, this drive lets you reinstall Windows RT if your Surface no longer starts on its own and all resuscitation efforts fail. To create a Recovery Drive, follow these steps:

1. From the Start screen, type **Create a Recovery Drive** and tap Settings from the Search pane.

2. Tap the Create a Recovery Drive link.

3. When the Recovery Drive window appears, follow the steps to insert your flash drive and create the Recovery Drive.

Stash the flash drive in a safe place. If Windows RT ever falters, you can insert the Recovery Drive as one of the troubleshooting steps I describe in Chapter 14.

When you turn on your Surface for the first time, you'll find app updates waiting for your Surface's bundled apps. And, if you've previously downloaded apps for another Windows 8 or Windows RT PC, the Store lets you download those apps again onto your Surface.

To download and install all app updates, follow these steps:

1. **From the Start screen, tap the Store tile.**

    The Store app appears.

2. **Tap the word Updates in Store app's upper-right corner.**

    The store lists all of your waiting updates, each selected with a check mark in their upper-right corners. And, in a bit of convenience, the Store app appears, showing its App bar along the bottom.

3. **Tap the Install icon from the Store app's App bar.**

    The Store app begins downloading and automatically updating your apps.

4. **If desired, download your previously installed apps.**

    If you've downloaded apps from any Windows 8 computer using your Microsoft account, the Store app remembers. To see a list of your previously downloaded apps in the Store, swipe your finger down from the screen's top and tap Your Apps. A list appears, showing all the apps you downloaded from the Store using your Microsoft Account.

To install them all, tap the Select All icon (or just tap the ones you want to install) and tap the Install button.

- I describe the Store and apps in Chapter 9.

- If you refresh or reset your Surface as a troubleshooting measure, these steps restock your Surface with all your previously downloaded apps.

Setting Up User Accounts

Unlike competing tablets, your Microsoft Surface lets you create accounts for different users. That lets several people use the same Surface, with all of their information being kept separate from each other.

Separate accounts make it easy to share a Surface among a family, for example. (You can even set up limited-access accounts for children.)

You can set up three types of accounts:

- **Microsoft account:** This links your account with Microsoft, letting you download apps and use many of Microsoft's services. If you own a Surface, you want a Microsoft account.

- **Local account:** Local accounts work fine when for simple work, letting you browse the web, and create files using Word, Excel, PowerPoint, and One Note. But you can't download any apps from the Microsoft Store without typing in a Microsoft account and password, and many of the Surface's bundled apps also require an account and password, too.

- **Guest account:** This handy temporary account gives you a way to let a friend borrow your tablet for a quick e-mail check *without* giving them access to any of your files.

To set up a new user account on your Surface (or to convert a Local account to a Microsoft account), follow these steps:

1. **From any screen, fetch the Charms bar and tap Settings.**

Swipe your finger inward from the screen's right edge and then tap the Settings icon. The Settings pane appears.

2. **Tap the Change PC Settings link.**

   The PC Settings page appears.

3. **From the left column, tap Users.**

   The PC Setting page's Users section appears, shown in Figure 3-6.

Your account

PC settings

Andy Rathbone
andyrathbone@live.com

Personalize

You can switch to a local account, but your settings won't sync between the PCs you use.

Switch to a local account

Users

More account settings online

Notifications

Sign-in options

Search

Change your password

Share

Create a picture password

General

Create a PIN

Privacy

Require a password after the display is off for

Devices

15 minutes ⌄

Wireless

Other users

Ease of Access

There are no other users on this PC.

Sync your settings

+ Add a user

HomeGroup

Figure 3-6: To add a new user account, tap Add a User from the bottom of the right column.

4. **Tap Add a User, and when the Add a User page appears, enter the new user's Microsoft account e-mail address, if they have one.**

   If they don't have a Microsoft account e-mail address, or you don't know it, tap Sign in Without a Microsoft Account from the bottom of the page. That takes you to a page where you can create a local account. To create a local account, just type in the new user's name and a simple password.

5. **If you're creating a Local account for a child, tap the check box labeled Is This a Child's Account? Turn on Family Safety to Get Reports of Their PC Use.**

Whether you create a Microsoft account or a Local account, that account's name then appears on the Sign On screen the next time you sign out of your account or turn on your Surface.

✔ To convert your Local account into a Microsoft account, follow the previous Steps 1-3. Then tap the Switch to a Microsoft Account button beneath your local account's name.

I cover Family Safety in Chapter 14.

✔ To turn on the Guest account, type **guest account** directly from the Start screen, and tap Settings from the Search pane along the right. Then tap Turn Guest Account On or Off. When the Manage Accounts window appears, tap the Guest account icon and tap the next page's Turn On button.

Turning Off Your Surface

This section really doesn't need to be here because you don't ever need to turn off your Surface. In fact, pushing the power button just puts it to sleep. It doesn't turn it off at all.

The Windows RT version can sleep for days before the batteries give out. While it's sleeping, a tap on the keyboard or a tap of its power button brings it back to life with all your apps still open, just the way you left it.

The Windows 8 Pro version, however, doesn't offer as much battery life. When its batteries give out at the day's end, a sleeping Surface with Windows 8 Pro copies the contents of its memory to its hard drive and then turns off. Plug it into the wall, turn it back on, and all of its apps will reopen, just the way you left it.

If you're desperate to save battery life, you can turn off your Surface by following these steps:

1. **Summon the Charms bar by sliding your finger in from the screen's right edge and tapping Settings.**

2. **When the Settings pane appears, tap the Power icon.**

3. **Choose Shut Down from the Power icon's pop-up menu.**

When turned off, both the RT and Pro versions take longer to start up than they do to reawaken from sleep mode. And when they return to life, you'll have to reopen your apps.

Chapter 4

The First Walkthrough of Surface

*I*f you've never experienced Windows 8, you're in for a surprise when you first turn on your Surface. No longer just a menu, Windows 8's Start screen works like an operating system of its own, containing nearly all the tools a Surface owner needs.

Designed for tablets like the Surface, Microsoft built the Start screen to be finger-friendly, yet information-packed. It serves up quick, informational tidbits with the least amount of effort. Just turn on your Surface, for example, and the Lock screen already shows your next appointment, your number of unread e-mails, and the strength of your Internet connection and battery.

If the Start screen lacks a tool you need for a particular task, visit the Windows Store (itself an app) and download an app to handle the job. *Apps* — small, touch-friendly programs — hail from the world of smartphones. In fact, a Surface works much like a smart phone with a larger screen.

This chapter explains how to get the most from Windows 8's Start screen and its bundled apps.

Unlocking and Signing In

When you turn on your Surface, the Start screen hides behind the Lock screen, shown in Figure 4-1. Yet even before you move past the Lock screen, your Surface already dishes up useful information.

Figure 4-1: The Lock screen shows the date, time, your next appointment, the strength of your battery and Internet connection.

At glance at the Lock screen's lower-left corner shows the current day, date and time, as well as the strength of your battery and wireless Internet connection. Plus, you can customize the Lock screen to show your next appointment, your number of unread e-mails, and other tidbits of information.

To move past the Lock screen, swipe up with your finger, right-click a mouse, or press any key on the keyboard. The screen slides up and off the screen, revealing the sign-on screen, shown in Figure 4-2, listing all your user accounts.

To sign in, tap your user account, and type in your password; Windows 8's tile-filled Start screen appears.

- ✔ When typing in any hidden password, you can tap the little eye icon at the end of the password line for a peek at what you've typed. It's a handy way to make sure you're typing in the correct password.

- ✔ Windows reminds you if your Caps Lock key is turned on, so you don't mistakenly type your password with uppercase letters.

✔ If you see the Guest account listed, feel free to let a friend enter it. The Guest account is handy for letting a friend temporarily sign on and check her e-mail. I describe how to turn on the Guest account in Chapter 3.

✔ I describe how to customize your Lock screen background and icons in Chapter 14.

Figure 4-2: To sign in with an account, tap its picture.

Windows 8's New Start Screen

If you've used Windows before, you're probably familiar with the Windows desktop. You've seen several open programs, each running inside its own resizable window.

That approach worked fine on desktop PCs with keyboards, mice, and large monitors. People could create spreadsheets and write reports for hours, all the while looking forward to lunchtime.

Tablets like your Surface, by contrast, serve different needs. Tablet owners don't create documents inside an office cubicle; they manipulate bits of information in a variety of ways. They fill out forms at job sites, for example, read books on the couch, or glance at a map while walking through a convention hall. Your Surface lets you do these tasks quickly, with your fingers, while on the go.

That's where Windows 8's new Start screen comes in, shown in Figure 4-3.

Figure 4-3: The Windows 8 Start screen includes "live" tiles, which constantly update to show the latest information.

Designed specifically for tablets, Windows 8's Start screen resembles a personalized billboard. Filled with colorful tiles, the Start screen spreads across your Surface's wide screen, extending off the right edge.

Each tile represents an *app* — a small program — and many tiles constantly percolate to bring up new information. Your Mail app's tile, for example, constantly cycles through your latest unread e-mails. The Weather app displays the ever-changing forecast for your location, and the Calendar app shows the time and location of your next appointment.

That's not to say you *can't* work on a Surface. Your Surface still includes the traditional Windows desktop — it's an app waiting to be opened, like everything else in Windows 8. Open the Desktop app with a tap on its tile, and your Surface's Start screen quickly clears to reveal the desktop, complete with its movable and resizable windows.

✔ To see the portion of the Start screen that disappears off the screen's right edge, slide your finger along the screen from right to left, just as if you were sliding a piece of paper. As your finger moves, the Start screen travels along with it, bringing more tiles into view.

✔ To scroll through the Start screen with your Touch or Type cover's trackpad, put two fingertips on the trackpad. Slide your two fingers to the left or right, and the Start screen follows them. (Your keyboard's cursor keys also scroll the screen: They let you jump from tile to tile.)

✔ Having trouble finding things on the Start screen? I explain how to organize your screen into neatly labeled groups later in this chapter.

 ✔ Need a new app to meet a particular need? I explain how to download and install new apps from the Windows Store in Chapter 7.

 ✔ I cover the Desktop app in Chapter 12. Microsoft worked hard to make the desktop finger-friendly. But if you're looking for the same level of productivity you had on a desktop PC, attach your Surface keyboard.

 ✔ Although the Desktop app is certainly convenient to have around, you probably won't load it too often. The Start screen apps serve most needs quite well.

Opening, Closing, and Switching between Apps

The Start screen heralds a new way of working with Windows and its ecosystem of small, inexpensive apps rather than large, expensive desktop programs.

To help you figure out this new world, this section covers app basics: How to open and close them, switch between them, and find their menus when they need a few tweaks.

Opening an app

When first installed, Windows 8 doesn't bother to organize your Start screen, shown earlier in Figure 4-3. Your apps appear in a haphazard mess that sprawls out of view beyond the screen's right edge. As you slide your finger along the Start screen from right to left, the tiles move, bringing more into view.

If you spot the app you'd like to open, tap it with a finger: The app fills the screen, ready for action.

However, the bigger task may be simply *finding* the app you want to open. The sprawling Start screen doesn't alphabetize your apps or organize them into manageable groups. That leaves way too many hiding places.

When your sought-after app is lost in a sea of tiles, bring the app to the surface by following these steps:

1. **Swipe up from the screen's top or bottom. When the Start screen's menu appears along the bottom edge, tap the All Apps icon.**

   The Start screen lists an alphabetical list of all your apps, shown in Figure 4-4, followed by a list of your desktop programs, organized alphabetically by category. Still don't spot the app you're after? Move to Step 2.

2. **Pinch the All Apps screen between two fingers.**

   The app icons disappear, and Windows lists the alphabet, from A to Z, shown in Figure 4-5. Tap the first letter of your lost app — J, perhaps — and Windows redisplays all the apps. This time, though, apps beginning with J are placed directly beneath your finger, making them easier to find.

   This trick works best for Start screen's with a huge variety of apps. If you *still* can't find your wayward app, move to Step 3.

3. **Search for the app.**

   Swipe your finger in from the right edge to fetch the Charms bar, covered later in this chapter. When the Charms bar appears, tap the Search icon. A box appears for you to type in the missing app's name. As you type, Windows lists matching apps, narrowing down the list with each letter you type.

   Spot your app? Tap its icon to launch it.

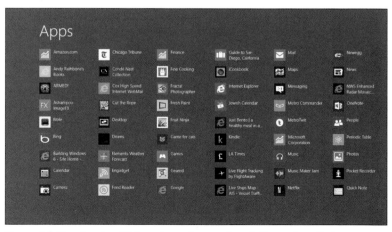

Figure 4-4: Tapping the All Apps icon shows a list of all your installed apps, alphabetized by category.

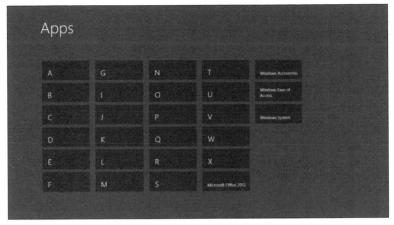

Figure 4-5: Pinch the list of all the apps, and Windows displays the alphabet and program categories.

If you've added a keyboard to your Surface, just begin typing the app's name directly onto the Start screen. The Start screen quickly transforms into a list of every app matching what you've typed so far. After you spot your app's name on the list, tap it, and it leaps onto the screen. (Or, if your typing has narrowed down the list to one app, press Enter on the keyboard to launch the app.)

- ✔ The Start screen never shows *all* of your installed apps. Unless you personally reorganize it, described at this chapter's end, the Start screen shows only the apps Microsoft chose to be listed.

- ✔ Want an unlisted app to appear on the Start screen? Put it there yourself: When looking at the app's tile from the All Apps layout shown in Figure 4-4, select the app by sliding its icon up or down a bit. (A check mark appears to let you know it's selected, and the bottom menu appears.) Then, tap the Pin to Start icon from the bottom menu.

- ✔ Still don't see an app that meets your needs? It's time to visit the Windows Store, a trip covered in Chapter 7.

Closing an app

Older versions of Windows always wanted you to *close* unneeded programs: You'd click on the little X in the program's upper-right corner, and the program disappeared from the screen.

You won't find any close buttons on apps, however: Apps aren't meant to be closed. When they're not being used, apps simply rest in the background, waiting in case you need them again. They consume very few resources, and they don't eat much, if any, battery power.

When you're done with an app, just head back to the Start screen by pressing the Windows key on the front of your Surface. (You can also swipe in from the screen's right edge and touch the Start icon on the Charms bar, covered later in this chapter.) Then load a different app and do something else.

But if you *want* to close an app, perhaps one that's making annoying noises in the background, it's not difficult:

To close the app currently filling your screen, slide your finger down from the screen's top edge all the way down to its bottom edge. As you slide, the app follows your finger, shrinking, and then disappearing completely when your finger reaches the screen's bottom edge.

It's oddly empowering to watch your finger pull that unwanted app off the screen. It's an easy trick to remember, and you'll find yourself wanting to do it again and again.

Switching between apps

When they're not being used, apps slumber in the background. Your Surface ignores them, devoting its full attention to the app currently filling the screen.

But if you want to awaken a previously used app, you can summon it with this easy trick:

To switch back to the app you've just used, swipe your finger inward from the Surface's left edge.

As your finger moves inward from the screen's edge, it drags your last-used app along with it. When you can see the app begin to appear onscreen, lift your finger: The app grows to fill the screen.

Keep repeating the same trick, sliding your finger in from the left, and you'll eventually cycle through *all* your currently open apps.

Can't remember whether an app's already open? To see a list of your last six open apps, follow these steps from any screen on your Surface:

1. **Slowly slide your finger inward from screen's left edge.**

2. **When you see an app begin to slide into view, slide your finger back to the left edge.**

   All of your opened apps appear in a column clinging to the screen's left edge, shown in Figure 4-6.

Figure 4-6: Swipe your finger in from the screen's left edge, and then slide it back slightly until a column of recently used apps aligns itself against the screen's left edge.

After you see the apps' thumbnails clinging to the screen's left edge, you can perform a few other circus tricks:

- ✓ **Return to an open app:** Tap an app's thumbnail from along the screen's left edge, and the app fills the screen. Simple.

- ✓ **Close an app:** With your finger, slide the app slightly to the right and then down and off the screen. This one takes practice, as the app tries to muscle its way onto the screen. (If you're using a Surface keyboard, right-click the unwanted app's thumbnail using the trackpad and choose Close from the pop-up menu.)

- ✓ **Remove the app column:** Because that column of recently used apps consumes some real estate, it closes by itself after you open one of its apps. But if you want to close it manually, just tap the currently open app. That brings Windows attention back to your current app and closes the column of apps.

Installing and uninstalling an app

You install apps through the Windows Store app. I describe how to install and uninstall apps in Chapter 7.

Understanding the Charms Bar

Although it sounds like something dipped in milk chocolate, the Windows 8 Charms bar is simply a menu. More than that, it's a tool that unites every portion of Windows 8. The all-powerful Charms bar lives *everywhere*: on the Start menu, within every app, and even on the Windows desktop itself.

However, the Charms bar remains out of sight until you summon it with this trick:

Slide your finger inward from any screen's right edge, and the Charms bar appears, shown in Figure 4-7. The Charms bar also fetches a notification in the screen's bottom-left corner, showing the current time and date, as well as the strength of your wireless signal and battery.

Time   Day and date   The Charms bar

Battery strength

Wireless strength

Figure 4-7: Swipe your finger in from the screen's right edge, and the Charms bar appears.

The Charms bar displays five handy icons, each described in the following sections.

Your Surface's Touch and Type keyboards feature keys dedicated to the Charms bar's all-important icons. Look along the top row for keys dedicated to Search, Share, Devices, and Settings. The fifth icon, the Windows key, lives to the left of your keyboard's spacebar.

Search

When you need to find something in the sea of text you're currently viewing, fetch the Charms bar with a finger swipe inward from the screen's right edge. Then tap the Search icon, shown in the margin.

The Search pane appears along the screen's right edge, with a Search box ready for you to type what you'd like to find. The Search icon provides a quick way to find a particular reference in your currently viewed website, a lost e-mail from within your Mail app, or even the forecast for a different city in the Weather app.

But Search isn't restricted to the app you're currently viewing. By tapping different items on the Search pane, you route your search to cover your entire Surface. The Search pane, shown in Figure 4-8, offers these areas:

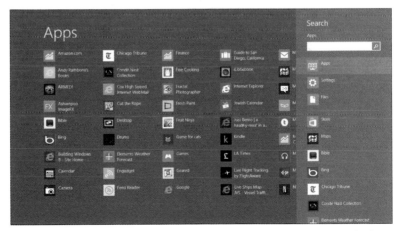

Figure 4-8: The Search command searches through what you're currently viewing. To search other areas, tap Apps, Settings, or Files.

- **Search box:** This lets you search what you're currently viewing, be it a website, app, or even a folder on the Windows desktop. Type what you're seeking inside this box, and then tap the Enter key. Below the Search box, you often see names of items you've searched for previously, letting you retrieve them again with a quick tap.

- **Apps:** Choose this to find an app you can't locate on the Start screen. As you type, a list of matching apps appears onscreen. When you spot your app, launch it with a tap on its name.

- **Settings:** A search in this box looks through every setting found in Windows' two control panels: the Start screen's PC Settings area, as well as the desktop's Control Panel. Sometimes it's the only way to find a helpful-but-rarely-used setting that's hidden deeply in the Control Panel's crevices.

- **Files:** Choose this to search through all the files on your computer, as well files you've stored on SkyDrive, Microsoft's online storage space covered in Chapter 6. Searching for files turns up songs, videos, documents, and photos, bringing a list of matching names to the forefront. When you spot the one you want, launch it with a tap.

The Start screen's Search feature works well at finding information quickly and on the fly.

When you need to search other areas, or search for more specific items, try these tips:

- When you open Search, a list of things you've previously sought appears along the bottom of the Search pane, saving you from retyping the app's name. Tap an item's name to search for it again.

- To route a search to the Internet, open Internet Explorer. Then summon the Charms bar, tap the Search icon, and type in your search. Microsoft's Bing search engine searches for what you need.

- To search files on your *homegroup* — other computers on your home network — tap Files. Then tap the downward pointing arrow next to the word Files in the screen's upper-left corner. When the drop-down menu appears, choose Homegroup instead of Files. That routes your search to computers on your home network's homegroup.

- When you need to do more advanced searches — finding files created on a certain date, perhaps — open the Desktop app. Just as with Windows Vista and Windows 7, every desktop folder includes a Search box in its upper-right corner. To fine-tune your searches, tap the Ribbon menu's Search tab and tap the type of search you need.

Share

Computers excel at sharing information. There's little point in creating something unless you want somebody else to see it. That's where the Charms bar's Share icon comes in.

When you're viewing something you want to share, fetch the Charms bar with a swipe of your finger inward along the Screen's right edge.

When the Charms bar appears, tap the Share icon, shown in the margin. The Share pane appears, listing different ways you can share what you're currently viewing. You'll almost always see one universal sharing mechanism: the Mail app. Choose the Mail app to e-mail what you're seeing to a friend.

Choose the Share icon while viewing a website, for example, to e-mail its link to a friend, shown in Figure 4-9.

Figure 4-9: Tap the Share icon while viewing a website, and then tap Mail to e-mail its link to a friend.

Not all apps support the Share command. If an app doesn't support it, there's no way to share that app's contents. And, unfortunately, the Windows desktop doesn't support the Charms bar's Share command.

Start

Perhaps the most rarely used portion of the Charms bar, tapping the Start icon always drops you off at the Start screen. Why is it rarely used? Because touching the Windows key on the front of your Surface does the same thing. So does touching the Windows key on your Touch or Type keyboards.

 You can also fetch the Charms bar by swiping your finger inward from the screen's right edge, and then tapping the Start icon, shown in the margin. The Start screen returns to the forefront, ready for you to launch another app.

If you're already on the Start screen, tapping the Start icon returns you to your last-used app.

Devices

 This oddly named Charms bar icon doesn't say "Print," but that's probably what you'll use it for most often. Tapping the Charms bar's Devices icon lists all the devices attached to your computer that can interact with what's on the screen.

Most of the time, that device will be your printer. (Or your *printers*, if you're connected to more than one.)

To print something from an app on your Surface, summon the Charms bar by swiping inward from your Surface's right screen, and then tapping Devices. When the list of available devices appears in the Devices pane, tap your printer's name. Adjust any settings the printer offers and tap the Print button.

I describe printers in more detail in Chapter 6.

You also tap the Charm bar's Devices icon to send your screen to a second monitor, also described in Chapter 6.

Settings

The Charms bar's Settings icon lets you tweak the settings of the app you're viewing, a perk when you're desperately looking for an app's menus, or need to adjust its boorish behavior. But the over-looked icon also serves as a gateway for tweaking many of your Surface's most common settings, as well. (Some apps even offer a Help menu here, as well.)

 To change your currently viewed app's settings, summon the Charms bar by sliding your finger in from the screen's right edge. When the Charms bar appears, tap the Settings icon. The Settings pane appears, shown in Figure 4-10.

Settings for your tablet

Settings for the currently viewed app

Settings pane

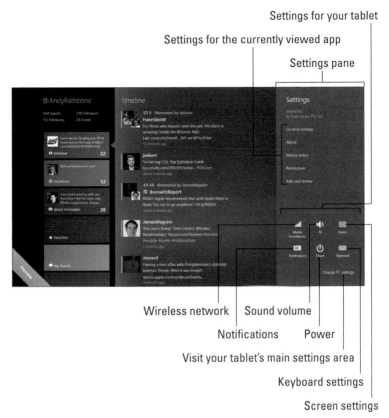

Wireless network | Sound volume

Notifications | Power

Visit your tablet's main settings area

Keyboard settings

Screen settings

Figure 4-10: The top of the Settings pane lists settings for your currently viewed app; the bottom lists shortcuts to other popular settings.

Along the top of the Settings pane, you see the settings available for the app you're currently viewing onscreen. And along the pane's bottom, you see these quick shortcuts to your Surface's most-tweaked settings:

✓ **Networks:** Look here for your wireless signal strength, as well as the name of the wireless connection that's currently pouring the Internet into your Surface. (Tap the icon to find the Airplane Mode toggle, which turns off wireless when you're on an airplane.)

✓ **Volume:** Tap here to fetch a sliding volume control. Slide the bar up to increase the sound; slide it down to lower it. (The dedicated keyboard keys on the Surface's Touch and Type keyboards do the same thing.)

✓ **Screen:** Tapping here brings a sliding control for screen brightness. (Tap the monitor icon atop the sliding control to lock your Surface's rotation control, keeping it from constantly moving right-side up.)

✔ **Notifications:** Designed for people tired of seeing notifications about Instant Messages and other informational tidbits popping up onscreen, this button lets you turn them off for one, three, or eight hours so you can get some work done.

✔ **Power:** Tap here to Sleep, Shut down, or Restart your Surface.

✔ **Keyboard:** This lets you switch between different keyboards or languages, as well as call up the onscreen keyboard, which is listed as Touch Keyboard and Handwriting Panel.

✔ **Change PC Settings:** Tap here to visit the Start screen's PC Settings area, a goldmine of settings for tweaking the Start screen to meet your particular needs. (Visit the PC Settings area's Personalize section, for example, to customize your Surface's Lock screen, Start screen, and your account picture.) I cover the PC Settings area in Chapter 14.

Organizing the Start Screen

For some reason, Windows 8 doesn't bother to organize your Start screen. As you add apps from the Windows Store, the Start screen tosses them onto its far right edge, where they're completely out of sight.

To combat the sprawl, organize your Start screen with this six-step plan. It only organizes your Start screen as much as you'd like. If you prefer working with a messy desk, stop after the first step or two. If you sort your pens by color in separate trays, follow these steps to the very end. That will transform your sprawling Start screen into an array of neatly labeled groups.

Follow these steps to organize your Start screen into something you can live with:

1. **Remove tiles for apps you don't want.**

When you spot an app you'll never use, get rid of it: Slide your finger down the tile slightly to select it. Then, from the menu that appears along the Start screen's bottom, tap Unpin from Start (shown in the margin). Repeat until you've removed all your unwanted app tiles.

Choosing Unpin from Start doesn't *uninstall* the app or program; it only removes the tile from the Start screen. If you accidentally remove a tile for a favorite app or program, you can easily put it back in the next step.

2. Add tiles that you *do* want.

Swipe your finger upward from the Start screen's bottom edge, and then tap the All Apps button along the screen's bottom. The Start screen disappears, showing icons for *all* your installed apps, listed in alphabetical order.

When you spot an app that you want to appear on the Start screen, select it with a quick downward slide of your finger. (A check mark appears in the app's upper-right corner to show that it's selected.)

Finally, tap the Pin to Start icon from the Start screen's bottom menu. Windows 8 tosses a tile for that app onto the Start menu's far right end.

You can select several apps simultaneously, and then tap the Pin to Start icon to place them all onto the Start screen.

3. Move related tiles closer to each other.

When related tiles appear next to each other, they're easier to find on the Start screen. For example, I like to keep my people-oriented apps — Mail, People, and Calendar — next to each other on the left edge for easy access.

To drag a tile from one place to another, select it first with a little downward drag, and then drag it to its new location. As your finger moves the tile, other tiles automatically move out of the way to make room.

When you've dragged an app's tile to the desired spot, lift your finger, and the tile remains in its new home.

If a rectangular tile consumes too much space, shrink it into a square: Select the tile with a slight downward slide, and then tap the Smaller button from the App menu along the Start screen's bottom. (Remember, though, some apps only have room to show live updates on larger, rectangular tiles. To return a tile to normal size, repeat these steps, but choose the Larger button.)

4. Move related tiles into groups.

Placing related tiles into separate groups makes them easier to relocate. For example, you may want to create one group for tiles you use at home, another for work-related tiles, and a third for tiles that play media — choose whatever groups work for you.

To begin creating new groups, look closely at your Start screen: It comes set up in two groups. (Look for an empty space separating the two groups.)

To create a new group, select a tile with a slight downward drag, and then drag that tile into the empty space that separates two groups. As your dragged tile reaches that empty space, the groups move farther apart, shown in Figure 4-11, and a bar appears between them. Lift your finger, and the tile drops into place, forming a new group.

Repeat this step, rearranging tiles and creating new groups until your related tiles live together in their own separate groups.

5. **Name the groups of related tiles.**

    After you've created groups or related tiles, give each group a name so you can easily identify its purpose.

    Start by pinching the Start screen tiles between two fingers; as you slide your two fingers closer together, the tiles shrink until you're looking at all of your groups onscreen, shown in Figure 4-12.

    Select a group with a slight downward slide of your finger. Then, from the bottom menu that appears, tap the Name Group icon. When the Name box appears, type in the group's name and tap the adjacent Name button to finish the job.

    Repeat until you've named all your groups.

Figure 4-11: Drag a selected tile between two groups; when the gray bar appears, lift your finger to drop the tile into place.

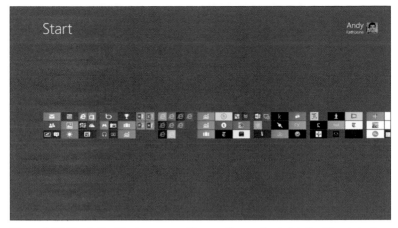

Figure 4-12: Pinch the Start screen with your fingers to shrink the tiles, bringing all your groups into view.

6. **Move groups so that your most important ones appear first.**

   While you're still looking at your groups as miniatures, shown in Figure 4-12, rearrange the groups by dragging them into new positions.

   Select a group with a slight downward slide of your finger; drag and drop the group into a different place.

   Repeat until your most frequently accessed groups of tiles appear on the far left.

When you finish dragging, dropping, and naming tiles and groups, your Start screen is customized to the way *you* use your Surface. Your tiles live in their own neatly named groups, and your most frequently accessed tiles appear first on the screen.

You can add favorite desktop folders and libraries to the Start screen, as well. While on the Desktop, hold down your finger on a desired folder or library; when a square appears, lift your finger. Then, from the menu that appears, tap Pin to Start.

Choosing Files with the File Picker

Eventually, you'll need to select a file from within a Start screen app. For example, you may want to open a photo to view in the Photos app. That's where the File Picker comes in. It's not much of a file management tool, but it works fine for selecting a few files or folders when needed.

Oddly enough, the File Picker can't be summoned on its own; there's no way to fetch it and simply browse your files. If you *do* want to browse files, head to the Desktop app and run File Explorer, as I describe in Chapter 12.

No, the File Picker can only be summoned from within a Start screen app. And when it appears, shown in Figure 4-13, you see that it's a bare-bones program, designed merely to navigate storage areas, and find file or two.

When the File Picker eventually rears its head on your Surface, follow these steps to locate a file:

1. **Tap the word Files in the screen's upper-left corner, and choose the storage area containing your file.**

   When you tap the word Files, a menu drops down, listing all the storage areas available on your Surface: your Documents, Pictures, Music and Videos libraries, for example, as well as your Windows desktop and your Downloads folder. (The Downloads folder contains all the files you download from websites.)

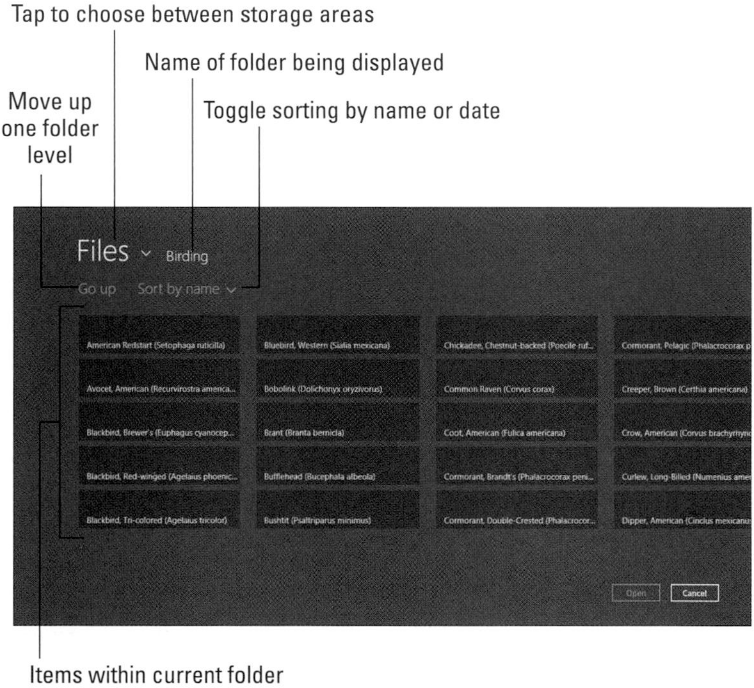
Tap to choose between storage areas
Name of folder being displayed
Move up one folder level
Toggle sorting by name or date
Files
Birding
Go up
Sort by name
Open
Cancel
Items within current folder

Figure 4-13: Some apps summon the File Picker to let you choose a file to view or change.

You can also access places outside of your Surface. You can access files shared on your homegroup from other networked PCs, as well as files stored on SkyDrive, which I cover in Chapter 6.

Some of your apps may have also added their storage spaces to the File Picker's menu, as well.

2. **Tap the folder or storage area you'd like to open, or tap the file you'd like to select.**

   When you tap a storage area in Step 1, the File Picker displays all of that storage area's folders and files. (To help you keep track of what you're seeing, the File Picker lists the name of the folder you're currently viewing next to the word Files, as shown in Figure 4-13.)

   If you see your file's name, tap it and you're through: Your app opens it.

   Tapped the wrong folder by mistake? Tap the words Go Up, just below the Files button, to return.

   If you don't see your desired file, keep tapping folders, opening different ones to keep looking.

Still can't find your file? Summon the Charms bar and tap the Search icon, described earlier in this chapter. Windows Search feature can find it fairly quickly. After you find it, remember its location, so you can return to it with the File Picker.

Using the Start Screen with a Mouse and Keyboard

If you plan on using the Desktop app to crank out some serious work, you'll want to attach your Surface's keyboard or plug in a mouse and keyboard, as I describe in Chapter 6. The mouse and keyboard feel right at home on the desktop, of course, but the Start screen is a different world.

Yet, the mouse and keyboard still let you navigate the Start screen, although a little more awkwardly. If you wish, you can simply use your fingers while navigating the Start menu; plugging in your keyboard or a separate mouse and keyboard won't disable the touch controls.

But if you'd prefer to leave your hands on your keyboard, trackpad, or mouse, Table 4-1 shows how to control the Start screen with a mouse and keyboard.

Table 4-1	Controlling the Start Screen with a Mouse and Keyboard	
How to . . .	*With a Mouse*	*With a Keyboard*
Open the Charms bar	Point at the screen's top or bottom-right corners	Win+C
Return to last-used app	Point at the screen's top-left corner and click	Win+Tab, Enter
Return to Start menu	Point at screen's bottom-left corner and click	Win
See currently running apps	Point at screen's top-left corner, and then slide the mouse downward	Win+Tab (keep pressing Tab to cycle through open apps)

Chances are, though, you'll still use your fingers on your Surface's screen even after plugging in a mouse and keyboard. You'll probably only use the keyboard for typing text, and the mouse for pointing at small items on the desktop.

Don't forget the dedicated Charms bar keys atop the Surface's Touch and Type keyboards. They let you jump quickly to the Charms bar's Search, Share, Devices, and Settings features.

Power users take note: If you right-click any screen's bottom-left corner, a power menu appears, covered at the end of Chapter 5. That menu places many oft-used settings a mouse-click away. (That secret menu is accessible only by clicking it with a mouse.)

Chapter 5

Typing, Touching, and Drawing on the Surface

Chances are, you know how to click a mouse, or manipulate a laptop's trackpad. A touchscreen adds a third dimension: Now, your *fingertips* alone tell your Surface how to behave. This chapter covers the touch control tricks stashed inside every Surface warrior's arsenal.

Here, you'll discover your Surface's seven main touch commands. Although these may sound complicated when reading them, envision your Surface's display as a piece of paper: Most of a Surface's finger commands are as intuitive as manipulating a sheet of paper as it lies flat on a table.

This chapter also explains the Surface's Touch and Type covers, letting you know the special finger commands and gestures built into its touchpad.

And because you may not have a keyboard, or your keyboard cover may be wrapped behind your Surface, I explain the mechanics of typing on the onscreen keyboard. Although unwieldy for most things, it's an excellent way to enter foreign characters and symbols.

Controlling a Touchscreen with Your Fingers

Controlling a touchscreen sounds easy enough. You just touch it, right? Complicating matters, though, is that your Surface's screen lets you touch it in *seven* different ways. And each type of touch does something very different.

This section describes the seven main ways to touch your Surface's screen, as well as examples of when to use each one.

Tap

The equivalent of a mouse click, this is a quick tap and release of your finger. You can tap any item on the screen, be it a button, icon, or other bit of computer viscera. When in tight quarters, a fingertip often works better than the pad of your finger.

Example: Tap the Next button to move to the next step; tap the Charms bar's Start button to return to the Start screen. Tap an app's tile on the Start screen to open the app.

Double-tap

The equivalent of a mouse's double-click, this is two quick taps of your finger. Double-tap any item on the screen that you'd like double-click on.

Example: Double-tap a desktop folder to open it. Double-tap a web page to make it larger.

On a Surface, many things can be opened by merely tapping. But if a tap doesn't open an item, try the double-tap instead.

Press and hold

The equivalent of a mouse's right-click on the Windows desktop, tap the item but *hold down your finger*. A second or two later, an square will appear onscreen. Lift your finger, and the square becomes a menu, just as if you'd right-clicked the item with your mouse.

Example: Press and hold your finger on a blank portion of the Windows desktop. When the square appears, lift your finger; a menu appears, letting you choose your desktop's settings.

Pinch and/or stretch

A handy way to zoom in or out of a photo or website, pinch the screen between two fingertips (usually your thumb and index finger). The photo, text, or window shrinks as your fingers move inward. (Lift your fingers when you've found the right size.)

To enlarge something, spread your two fingers across the screen. As your fingers spread, the object beneath them grows along with their movements.

Example: Stretch your fingers across hard-to-read items like web pages, photos, and documents until they reach a suitable level of size or detail. Pinch them to reduce their size and to fit more of them onto the screen.

Rotate

Press and hold the screen with two fingers and then rotate your fingers. The item turns as if it were paper on a table.

Example: When viewing maps or photos, rotating your two fingers repositions them according to your fingers' movements.

Slide

Press your finger against the screen, and then, without lifting your finger, slide your finger across the glass. When you lift your finger, the item stays in its new location.

Example: To reposition a window across the desktop, press your finger on the window's *Title bar* — that colored strip along its top edge. Slide your finger to the window's desired position, and then lift your finger to drop the window in its new place.

Swipe

Slide the finger a short distance in a certain direction, usually inward from one of the screen's edges. You'll constantly find yourself swiping inward from your Surface's edges throughout Windows 8, as that summons hidden menus.

Example: Swipe across a digital book to turn its pages. Swipe across a web browser's screen to scroll up or down a web page. Swipe across the Start menu to see tiles hidden along the left or right edges. Swiping almost always seems natural.

Note: You can also swipe to *select* items. To do that, swipe in the opposite direction the item usually moves. For example, the Start screen scrolls to the left or right. So, to select a particular Start screen tile, swipe it *downward* and release. Windows highlights the tile, and places a check mark in its top-right corner, meaning you've selected it for further action. (I describe the Start screen in Chapter 4.)

Typing with the Touch and Type Covers

Part of the Surface's attraction comes from its two keyboard covers. Thin and lightweight, they click onto the Surface with magnets. The connectors also let the keyboards draw power from the Surface, so they don't need batteries.

After you attach the keyboard, you can fold it in different directions to handle different tasks:

- Fold the keyboard down flat on a table, and you're ready to type. (Flip your Surface's kickstand back to keep it upright.)
- Fold the keyboard up to protect the screen, and you're ready to travel. (The Surface automatically goes to sleep.)
- Fold the keyboard around the back of your Surface, and it's out of the way, letting you control the Surface with your fingers. (The keyboard automatically turns off.)

A sensor embedded in the keyboard lets the Surface know its position so it can behave correctly. When flat on the table, the keyboard turns on, ready for you to type. When folded back behind the screen, the keyboard turns off. And when you close the keyboard, the Surface goes to sleep to preserve battery life.

Both keyboards also include a thin trackpad that lets you control a mouse pointer, clicking, double-clicking, and right-clicking.

The two keyboards both offer the usual typewriter keys, Function keys, and dedicated keys that bring up the Charms bar icons, control the volume, and pause or resume your music and video.

TIP

When you attach either keyboard, the screen's rotation lock automatically kicks in, keeping your Surface locked in landscape mode. Fold the keyboard behind the screen, and the rotation lock turns off, letting the screen rotate "right-side up" as you carry it around.

This section describes how the two covers differ and how to best put them to work.

The Surface Touch keyboard cover

Only 3 millimeters thick, the $130 Touch keyboard cover lacks mechanical keys. But its pressure-sensitive keys, shown in Figure 5-1, work surprisingly well. A mere touch won't trigger the keys, so you can rest your fingers on the keys without typing. But when you start tapping on the keys, the keyboard translates your taps into typing.

Figure 5-1: The Surface Touch keyboard doesn't move when touched.

The Touch keyboard feels almost like fabric or cardboard more than a keyboard, and typing on it is an eerie feeling at first. You can start typing on it immediately with good results, but your speed won't pick up until you've used it for a few days.

Don't try to type too quickly — you'll need to grow used to typing without feeling anything in response. But after you grow used to it, you'll find it faster than the onscreen keyboard. And unlike the onscreen keyboard, it doesn't cover half your screen.

Basically, the Touch keyboard works much like any other keyboard, but these tips will save you some time:

✔ The F and J keys have slight indentations on them to help you position your fingers correctly. Always feel for them with your index fingers, and your other fingers will stay aligned more correctly.

✔ The Touch keyboard isn't waterproof enough to toss into the dishwasher, but a damp rag removes most spills.

✔ The 12 dedicated keys across the keyboard's top edge double as Function keys. Although they're not marked, the Mute key is F1, and the PgDn key is F12. To turn a key into a Function key, hold down the Fn key while pressing it. (The Fn key is to the right of the spacebar.)

✔ The trackpad's left- and right-click buttons are just *beneath* the trackpad, separated by the little vertical line.

✔ If the mouse pointer or cursor disappears while you use the scroll pad, detach the keyboard, wait a few seconds, and reattach it. The pointer or cursor should reappear.

✔ The Touch keyboard comes in different colors: black, white, red, cyan, and magenta. (Not every country carries every color.) And no, snapping a colored keyboard onto your Surface won't automatically change your screen's background color to match. (I explain how to change your background color in Chapter 14.)

The Surface Type keyboard cover

The Surface's Type keyboard cover, shown in Figure 5-2, contains mechanical keys. Designed for people who prefer movable keys, this makes the keyboard two millimeters thicker than the Touch keyboard, a compromise readily accepted by many touch typists.

The Type keyboard cover weighs less than an ounce more than the Touch cover and costs only ten dollars more. If you feel hesitant about the immobile Touch cover, opt for the Type keyboard.

In addition to its movable keys, the Type keyboard differs from the Touch keyboard in a few other ways:

✔ The dedicated keys across the Touch keyboard's top row also list their Function key number, sparing you from having to count the keys to figure out which one is F5.

✔ The trackpad clicks when pressed, making it easier to tell when you right-click or left-click an item.

   ✔ The F and J keys have standard bumps rather than indentations
     to help you position your fingers.

   ✔ The Type keyboard only comes in a boring black color. Yawn.

Figure 5-2: The Surface Type keyboard offers mechanical keys that move when
touched.

Surface trackpad gestures

Both the Touch and the Type keyboards include a trackpad below
the keyboard. Chances are, you won't use it much: It's easier to
simply touch the Surface to do what you want.

However, it comes in handy if you spend much time on the desktop.
There, the trackpad controls your mouse pointer, bringing the
pinpoint precision needed to navigate the desktop's crowded
menus.

Table 5-1 explains how to mimic mouse clicks, drags, and scrolls
with your Surface's trackpad.

Table 5-1	Surface Trackpad Gestures
To do this . . .	*Do This*
Move the onscreen pointer	Drag your finger anywhere on the trackpad.

To do this . . .	Do This
Left-click	Tap one finger anywhere on the trackpad or press the left trackpad button.
Right-click the Windows desktop	Tap two fingers anywhere on the trackpad or press the right trackpad button.
Left-click and drag	Hold down the left trackpad button and then slide a finger in any direction. Or, tap and then tap and slide one finger in any direction.
Scroll	Slide two fingers horizontally or vertically.
Show an Start screen app's App bar	Tap two fingers anywhere on the trackpad.

Pay particular attention to these tips, which work equally well on both the Touch and Type keyboard's trackpads:

- ✔ When reading a website or browsing an app like the News app, put *two* fingers on the trackpad and then slide them back and forth or up or down, depending on how the page flows. That can often scroll the page more smoothly than touching the screen with your fingers.

- ✔ Tapping with two fingers brings up the right-screen menu on the desktop. That's often faster and easier than right-clicking by tapping on the trackpad.

- ✔ Tapping with two fingers quickly brings up an App's menu. But because you still need to tap the menu item with a finger or well-placed mouse click, it rarely saves time.

Typing on the Onscreen Keyboard

Your Surface isn't really complete without a Touch or Type keyboard cover. Combined with the Surface's built-in kickstand, a keyboard cover transforms your Surface into a laptop whenever you sit down.

But whether you own a keyboard or not, this section describes how to use the free keyboard built into every Surface: the *onscreen keyboard*, also called the virtual or glass keyboard. (Microsoft's menus sometimes refer to the onscreen keyboard as the Touch keyboard, not to be confused with the Surface's Touch keyboard cover.)

The onscreen keyboard will never outperform a *real* keyboard for speed. But with practice, your typing speed will improve. The rest of this section helps you make the most out of the keyboard found in every Surface tablet.

Summoning the onscreen keyboard

If you've attached your Touch or Type keyboards, the onscreen keyboard stays hidden. But when your keyboard is detached or folded behind your Surface, the onscreen keyboard is ready for action.

To type something on Windows 8's new Start screen or its apps, tap in the area where you'd like to type. As you tap, the onscreen keyboard automatically fills the screen's bottom half, shown in Figure 5-3, ready for you to begin typing.

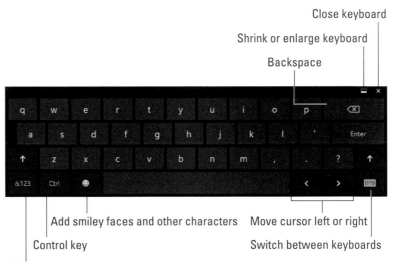

Close keyboard

Shrink or enlarge keyboard

Backspace

Add smiley faces and other characters   Move cursor left or right

Control key   Switch between keyboards

Add numbers and symbols from keyboards top row, as well as numeric keypad

Figure 5-3: While working within a Start screen app, tap where you'd like to type, and the onscreen keyboard appears.

 The Windows desktop isn't as friendly, unfortunately; tapping in a text box doesn't automatically summon the onscreen keyboard. You must *manually* summon the keyboard by tapping the keyboard icon (shown in the margin) on the taskbar along the desktop's bottom edge.

The keyboard looks and behaves much like a real keyboard, with many of the same keys. Position your fingers over the keys the

best you can and start typing. As you type, the letters appear onscreen.

Typing on glass is completely foreign to many people, and it's an oddly unsettling experience. Try these tips when typing for the first few days:

- ✔ Tap the Shift key to type an uppercase letter. (The Shift key automatically turns off after you've typed that first letter.) To turn on the Shift Lock, tap the Shift key twice. When you're through typing uppercase letters, tap the Shift key again to turn off Shift Lock.

- ✔ If you're accustomed to pressing keyboard commands like Ctrl+V for Paste, press the Ctrl key, and some of the keyboard's keys will change. The word *Paste* appears on the V key, for example. Other keys sprout labels, as well, letting you know which key you need to press to Select All, Undo, Cut, Copy, or Paste.

- ✔ Need a numeric keypad? Press the &123 key in the bottom-left corner, and the keypad appears, along with a Tab key and the brackets and symbols usually found on most keyboards' top row.

- ✔ When you're through typing, remove the keyboard from view, if necessary, by pressing the X in the keyboard's upper-right corner. The keyboard vanishes, leaving you with a full-screen view of your work in progress.

Switching between the four different onscreen keyboards

The onscreen keyboard normally looks like the one shown earlier in Figure 5-3. But the onscreen keyboard can morph into other keyboards, as well.

To switch to a different keyboard, press the Switch Keyboards button in the keyboard's bottom-right corner to switch between each of Windows 8's keyboards, shown in Figure 5-4.

Here are your other keyboard choices:

- ✔ **Thumb keyboard:** Built for a generation raised on smartphones, this peculiar keyboard lets you hold your Surface vertically, like a giant phone. The keyboard appears in two halves, each clinging to a bottom edge. Your left and right thumbs can then poke at the letters while typing, letting you whip out e-mails beneath the dinner table at family gatherings.

✔ **Handwriting:** Your Surface also recognizes your handwriting, translating it into text as you write on the screen, as I describe in this chapter's last section. However, writing or drawing requires a *stylus* — a type of pen with a special plastic tip.

The Surface with Windows 8 Pro includes a stylus, but the Windows RT version doesn't. However, any *capacitive* stylus (the cheap kind) works on the Surface RT.

✔ **Standard keyboard:** If you need a standard keyboard, complete with numbers and Function keys across the top, choose this keyboard. It's the real deal, complete with the Windows key, the Alt key, and even four arrow keys for navigating menus.

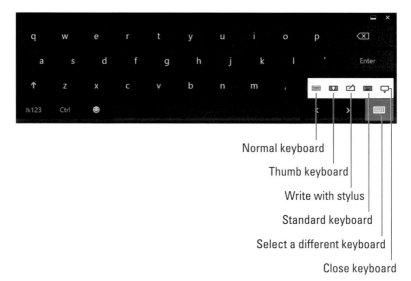

Normal keyboard

Thumb keyboard

Write with stylus

Standard keyboard

Select a different keyboard

Close keyboard

Figure 5-4: Tap the keyboard switching button to choose between Windows 8's four ways of entering text.

The Standard keyboard doesn't include a PrintScreen key. To take a screenshot on your Surface, hold down the Windows key on the Surface's front and press the Volume Down switch on the side. The screenshot appears as a PNG file in your Pictures library's Screenshots folder.

Typing special characters

Your Surface's onscreen keyboard makes it really easy to enter symbols and foreign characters, something quite difficult on other keyboards, including the Surface's Type and Touch keyboards.

To add the little hat on the letter é, for example, press and hold the onscreen keyboard's **e** key. A little pop-up appears around the letter, shown in Figure 5-5, showing possible foreign characters based on the e key: è, ē, é, ê, ë. Slide your finger in the direction of the key you want and let go. The desired key appears.

Figure 5-5: Press and hold a letter to see the possible variations and then slide your finger toward the character you want.

Holding down the question mark key lets you choose among eight other common symbols, including the semicolon, colon, brackets, hyphen, ampersand, and question mark.

Press the numbers key to bring up the number's keyboard. When the numbers keyboard appears, press the arrow keys directly above it to toggle between more characters, including symbols for copyright, mathematics, and popular currencies.

Editing Text

Without the pinpoint precision of a mouse pointer, editing a few lines of text seems insurmountable. How do you place the cursor in the exact location necessary to excise the unwanted text?

Like nearly anything else on your Surface, it starts with a strategically placed tap.

Double-tap a word near where you want to edit. Windows highlights the word, surrounding it with a small marker on each side. To extend the selection, drag the first marker to the selection's beginning; drag the second market to the section's end, as shown in Figure 5-6.

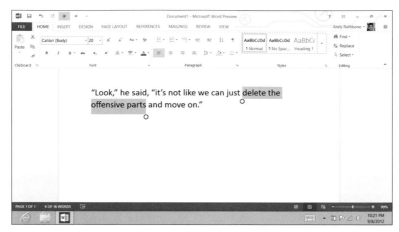

Figure 5-6: Tap a word to select it. Drag the markers until you've surrounded the portion you'd like to delete and then press the keyboard's Delete key to remove the unwanted text.

Different apps and programs often vary in how they treat a tap of your finger:

- ✔ Sometimes double-tapping a word highlights it, but doesn't place the markers on each side. If this happens, hold down the Shift key: As you slide your finger, Windows highlights adjacent words. When you've highlighted the desired words, left your finger and press Delete to delete them.

- ✔ Sometimes a tap simply places a cursor on the screen. Then you can drag the marker to the right or left until it's at the position where you'd like to begin typing.

- ✔ Having trouble putting the cursor where you want it? Try zooming in with your fingers: Straddle the words with your fingertips and then spread your fingers. In many programs, the text increases in size, making it much easier to touch *exactly* where you want to begin typing or editing.

- ✔ If your Surface came with a stylus, keep it handy. You can quickly and easily mark text for changes by drawing over it with your stylus, much like using a highlighter.

Drawing and Writing with a Stylus

When Microsoft first released tablets a decade ago, the company thought people would treat them as digital notepads: Doctors would carry them from room to room, scribbling notes, consulting charts, and viewing x-rays taken minutes before. That dream never quite caught on.

Instead, people today think of tablets as easy ways to watch movies, read books, or browse websites. Yet, all of Microsoft's pioneering "digital notepad" work isn't lost. Your Surface still accepts your handwriting when you draw on it with a *stylus* — a specially designed, plastic-tipped pen.

Because both models of Surface accept a stylus, you can write by hand anywhere that Windows accepts typing. You can handwrite a letter in Microsoft Word, for example, or write in the name of a newly created folder.

As you write, Windows converts your handwriting to words and drops them into the appropriate place.

The key is to call up the handwriting panel by following these steps:

1. **Tap where you'd like to enter text.**

   Tap any place that accepts text — an e-mail, a Word document, an entry in a calendar — even the name of a new file you're saving.

2. **If the handwriting panel doesn't appear, tap the taskbar's keyboard icon, shown in the margin.**

3. **If a keyboard appears instead of the handwriting panel, tap the keyboard switching key and choose the Stylus option, shown in the margin.**

   The handwriting panel appears.

4. **Begin writing in the handwriting panel, in cursive, block letters, or a combination.**

   As you write, Windows quickly begins recognizing the separate words, listing them in order along the panel's left edge. After you've written a short phrase, tap the Insert button. Windows inserts the words as text, shown in Figure 5-7.

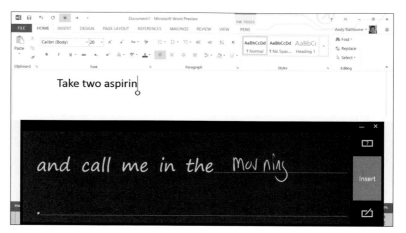

Figure 5-7: Tap the Insert button to insert your recognized words as text.

If all goes according to plan, you'll write your words, insert them, and move on. To bring yourself up to speed, tap the little question mark inside the rectangle (shown in the margin). Tiny visual tutorials show how to correct, delete, split, and join handwritten words.

The Surface with Windows RT requires a *capacitive* stylus, the inexpensive type of stylus sold nearly anywhere. (The ones sold for an iPad work fine.)

The Surface Pro, by contrast, comes with its own bundled *digitizer* stylus. More expensive than the capacitive stylus, the digitizer stylus allows finer, pressure-sensitive control when drawing. The Surface with Windows Pro includes a special screen with palm-blocking technology that makes it easier to take notes.

Both types of styli work in drawing programs, including Office OneNote, and the bundled desktop program called Paint.

Chapter 6

Connecting to the Internet, Printers, Monitors, Storage, and More

....

....

*Y*our Surface tablet strips computing down to the bare essentials: your data, a screen, and your fingers to control it all. You end up carrying a package weighing less than two pounds.

Yet your Surface can still adapt to meet your needs. Need to leave a paper trail? Plug in a printer. The Surface with Windows 8 Pro automatically recognizes most of them; a Surface with Windows RT recognizes many.

Need to crank out some Excel spreadsheets or a Word document, but don't have a Surface keyboard? Plug in a desktop PC mouse and keyboard and fire up the Desktop app. Screen too small? Plug in an external monitor.

Need more storage space? Slip in a memory card, plug in a flash drive, or even attach a portable hard drive. The list goes on: To watch high-definition movies in style, plug in an HDTV.

When you're through with all the accessories, unplug them and walk away. You've returned to minimalist mode, carrying all of your data with you.

That's the beauty of a Surface tablet.

Connecting to the Internet

Windows lives and breathes through the Internet, and if you're not connected, your programs will start to complain. Some Internet-starved programs offer helpful messages like "You're Not Connected." Other apps simply freeze, hoping you'll notice the tiny word "Offline" in their upper-right corners.

All Surface tablets can connect to the Internet *wirelessly* — they already contain a built-in wireless network adapter. To connect, you and your Surface need only be within range of a wireless network.

Today, that's easier than ever. You'll find Wi-Fi networks — sometimes called *hotspots* — waiting for you in airports, coffee shops, hotels, and many homes. (I describe how to set up your own home's wireless network in *Windows 8 For Dummies* also published by John Wiley & Sons, Inc.)

These steps explain how to know when you're within range of a Wi-Fi network, as well as how to connect to it and start browsing the Internet.

1. **From any screen, summon the Charms bar by sliding your finger inward from the screen's right edge.**

   When the Charms bar appears along the screen's right edge, look at the dark rectangle that also appears near the screen's bottom left. A glance at the icon in the rectangle's upper-left corner, shown in Figure 6-1, shows when you're within range of a wireless network.

A Wi-Fi network is available

No Wi-Fi network available

Figure 6-1: When you summon the Charms bar, this icon lets you know whether you're within range of a Wi-Fi signal.

If you're within range, move to Step 2. Not within range? Move to another spot, hopefully one with clusters of people huddled over their tablets and laptops.

2. **Tap the Charms bar's Settings icon. When the Settings pane appears, tap the Network icon.**

   The bottom of the Settings pane, shown in Figure 6-2, shows six icons. The icon in the top left represents networks. The icon toggles between Available and Unavailable depending on whether you're currently within range of a wireless network.

   • **Available:** When the icon says Available (shown in the margin), you're within range of a wireless network. Move to Step 3 to begin connecting.

   • **Unavailable:** When the icon says Unavailable (shown in the margin), you're out of range and out of luck. (Wi-Fi signals rarely reach more than 300 feet from their transmitter.) Try moving to a different location or ask somebody if there's a Wi-Fi signal available. Then return to Step 1.

3. **Tap the Available icon, if present.**

   The Settings pane turns into the Network pane, shown in Figure 6-3, listing the names of all the wireless networks around you. Depending on your location, you may see several listed. Windows ranks the wireless networks by signal strength, placing the strongest (and usually closest) network atop the list.

Tap this icon to connect to a wireless network

Figure 6-2: Amid the cluster of icons in the bottom of the Settings pane, tap the one in the top-left corner. (The icon usually says Available.)

Figure 6-3: Your Surface lists all the Wi-Fi networks within range. To connect to a network, tap its name.

A wireless network name's is known as its *SSID* (Service Set IDentification). The SSID represents the name that you (or the network's owner) chose when originally setting up the wireless network.

4. Tap the name of the network you'd like to connect to and tap the Connect button that appears.

If you'll be connecting to this network frequently, tap the Connect Automatically check box before tapping the Connect button, both shown in Figure 6-4. That tells your tablet to connect automatically whenever you're within range, a convenience you'll enjoy in your home, office, or favorite coffee shops.

If Windows connects to the network, you've finished: You've connected to an *open network*, meaning it's unsecured and requires no password. (Don't do any shopping or banking on an unsecured network.)

If Windows asks you to enter a password, however, move to Step 5.

5. Enter the password for the wireless network and tap the Next button.

If Windows asks you to Enter the Network Security Key when you tap the Connect button, you're trying to connect with a *secured*, or password-protected network. So, you must type in the network's password, shown in Figure 6-5.

Figure 6-4: When your Surface lists names of all the Wi-Fi networks within range, connect to one by tapping its name and tapping the Connect button.

Tap and hold the Eyeball icon to reveal password

Figure 6-5: Type in the network's password and tap Next.

If you're in your own home, here's where you type in the password you created when setting up your wireless network. (On some wireless routers, you can simply press a button on the router at this point, which proves you're in the same room.)

If you're connecting to somebody *else's* wireless network, by contrast, then you need to ask the network's owner for the password. (Or whisper "What's the Wi-Fi password?" to the person next to you at the coffee shop.)

TIP

Windows hides the password as you type it, keeping it secure from nearby eyes. Think you've made a typo? Then tap and hold the eyeball icon on the right side of the password field, shown in Figure 6-5, and Windows displays your password. (That handy eyeball icon appears whenever you type hidden passwords into a Start screen app.)

6. **Choose whether you want to share your Surface's files on the network.**

   This important choice, shown in Figure 6-6, depends whether you're connecting in a *private* setting, like your home or office, or a *public* location, like a hotel or coffee shop.

   - **Private:** If you're at your home or office, tap Yes, Turn on Sharing and Connect to Devices. That lets you connect with networked printers and swap files with other people on the network.

   - **Public:** Because you don't want strangers to access your files, tap No, Don't Turn on Sharing or Connect to Devices. That lets you access the Internet, but keeps other people on the network away from your files.

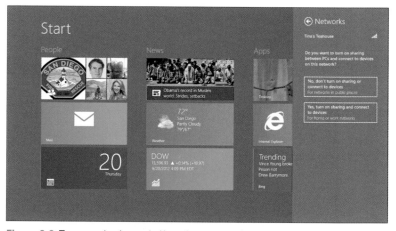

Figure 6-6: Turn on sharing only if you're connecting to your own network.

When you finish the steps, Windows connects to the network and your Internet connection begins flowing into your Surface. If the Internet connection remains dry, however, try these things:

✔ **Move closer to the transmitter.** This often-difficult maneuver cures 90 percent of Wi-Fi connection problems. Ask somebody where the Wi-Fi transmitter is located, or look for the small plastic box with two pencil-sized antennas sticking up from it. (They're often mounted on walls or atop cabinets.)

Disconnecting for airplane mode

Airplane mode is shorthand for disconnecting completely from the Internet. To put your Surface into Airplane mode before a plane flight, follow these steps:

1. **Summon the Charms bar by swiping your finger in from the screen's right edge, and then tap the Settings icon.**

2. **When the Settings pane appears, tap the Network icon.**

3. **When the Network pane appears, tap the Airplane Mode toggle switch along the pane's top edge.**

The Settings pane's Network icon shows that you're in Airplane mode. (Bluetooth wireless gadgets, covered later in this chapter, also stop working in Airplane mode.) To turn off Airplane mode and return to a lifestyle of searching for Internet connections, repeat the three steps.

✔ **Try connecting to an unsecured network.** They work fine for casual browsing.

✔ **You can also connect to a wireless network from the Windows desktop.** When the taskbar's right corner shows a wireless network available icon (shown in the margin), tap it. That takes you to Step 4 in the previous list for you to choose a network and tap the Connect button.

Windows RT tablets connect to the Internet through wireless networks. If you need cellular access, you can connect through a cell phone, known as *tethering*, or rent a portable Wi-Fi hotspot from a cellular carrier.

Surface with Windows 8 Pro tablets, by contrast, aren't limited to Wi-Fi Internet connections. They can also connect to wired networks with USB-to-Ethernet adapters and dial-up networks with USB-to-Dial-Up adapters.

To disconnect from a wireless network, simply walk out of range; Windows disconnects automatically. Or, if you want to disconnect while still in range, summon the Charms bar, tap the Settings icon, tap the Network icon, tap the network's name, and tap the Disconnect button.

Connecting to Networked PCs

Your Surface's hard drive may always seem too small, at least by desktop PC standards. Because you probably can't fit all of your information onto your Surface, keep an eye out for other places to stash files, storing a few videos in one spot and a few music files someplace else.

One of the easiest places to stash your files might be on your home or office network. To browse the files on those huge-hard-drive-stuffed PCs, you first need to connect to their wireless network.

To connect to PCs on a home or office network, follow the steps in the previous section to connect to their wireless network. In the last step, though, make sure to tap the button called Yes, Turn On Sharing and Connect to Devices.

But what if you forgot to tap that Sharing and Connect button?

You can turn it on by following these steps. These steps also let you connect to a *homegroup* — a simple way for Surface tablets, Windows 7, and Windows 8 computers to share files.

1. **Summon the Charms bar by sliding your finger in from your Surface's right edge and then tap the Settings icon.**

2. **Tap your wireless network icon.**

3. **When the Network pane appears, listing your connected wireless network, hold your finger on the network's name. When a circle appears, lift your finger.**

   Holding down your finger on an item until a menu appears is the equivalent of right-clicking with a mouse. In this case, the right-click menu appears, shown in Figure 6-7.

4. **Tap Turn Sharing On or Off, shown in Figure 6-7.**

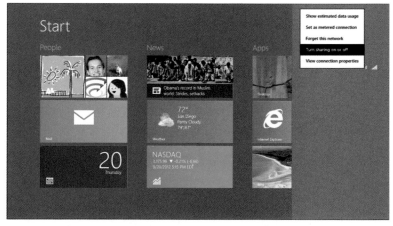

Figure 6-7: Tap Turn Sharing On or Off to either share files or stop sharing files on a network.

The permission screen you saw earlier, shown in Figure 6-7, presents itself again.

That right-click menu offers other handy options, which I describe in this chapter's sidebar, "Changing your Wi-Fi connection's settings."

5. **Tap the button Yes, Turn on Sharing and Connect to Devices.**

    Now that you've turned on sharing, join your network's homegroup, if you have one.

6. **Tap the Start screen's Desktop app, and then tap the File Explorer icon.**

    You find the icon for File Explorer (shown in the margin) near the left end of the *taskbar* — the strip along the bottom of the desktop. (I cover File Explorer in Chapter 12.)

7. **When File Explorer appears, tap the word Homegroup from the Navigation pane that clings to every folder's left edge.**

    The Homegroup window appears.

8. **Tap the Join Now button, shown in Figure 6-8, and follow the steps to enter the homegroup's password.**

Don't know the homegroup's password? To find it, visit any computer on the homegroup, open any folder, and right-click the word *Homegroup* from the Navigation pane. When the pop-up menu appears, choose View the Homegroup Password. That's the password you need to enter into your Surface.

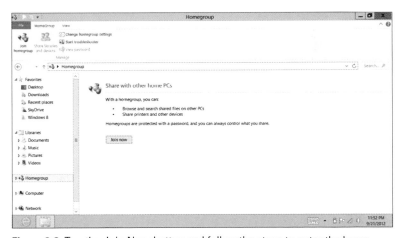

Figure 6-8: Tap the Join Now button and follow the steps to enter the homegroup's password.

✔ In Step 8 in the preceding list, clicking Next at each window lets you connect to the homegroup and begin access the contents of the Pictures, Videos, and Music libraries on other computers in the homegroup.

✔ Although the Surface with Windows RT can connect to an existing homegroup and access files from those computers, it can't create a new homegroup, nor will it let other homegroup computers access its own files. (The Surface with Windows 8 Pro doesn't have this restriction.) Tablets with Windows RT may not be able to print to some of the network's shared printers.

✔ Joining a homegroup also lets you connect with many networked devices (usually, printers). The Windows 8 Pro tablets can share the contents of their pictures, videos, and music libraries. The Documents folder on all homegroups remains private and not shared.

✔ Store things you want to share from your desktop PC in your libraries: Music, Pictures, and Videos. That makes them available to your Surface, as well as any Windows 7 and Windows 8 PCs on the network's homegroup.

✔ Although Windows Vista and Windows XP PCs can't join homegroups, you can access their files from your Surface in another way from Windows RT and Windows 8 Pro tablets. Tap the word Network at the bottom of any folder's Navigation pane. The Network window appears, listing every networked PC. Tap any PCs name to open it and browse its shared files.

Connecting to a Printer

Tablets running Windows 8 Pro can connect with just about any printer that works with your desktop PC.

Surface tablets with Windows RT, by contrast, are pickier about their printers. They allow drivers to be installed only through Windows Update, which means you can't simply run a printer's installation program. Many newer printers work, but you may have trouble connecting with older printers.

Most printers connect either through a USB port or through a wired-or-wireless network.

✔ **USB:** The simplest way to connect with a USB printer is to plug the printer's USB cable directly into your Surface's USB port.

✔ **Network and wireless:** After you create a network, described in a previous section, your Surface has access to all the printers shared on that network.

Changing your Wi-Fi connection's settings

Windows 8 offers many handy ways to change or keep track of your Wi-Fi network's settings. However, it's difficult to find the right switches until you follow these steps:

1. **Summon the Charms bar by sliding your finger in from your Surface's right edge, and then tap the Settings icon.**

2. **Tap your wireless network icon.**

3. **When the Network pane appears, listing your currently connected wireless network, hold your finger on the network's name until a square appears; lift your finger.**

   The equivalent of right-clicking with a mouse, that action brings a pop-up box with these options:

✔ **Show Estimated Data Usage:** Designed for people with metered cellular data plans, this toggle switch displays how many megabytes of data have flowed through your connection. To return your counter to zero, tap the Reset button.

✔ **Set as Metered Connection:** Choose this if you're on a *tiered* data plan, which limits the amount of data you can upload or download. Enter your limit in this area, and Windows warns you when you're about to surpass your limit. Plus, Windows automatically switches to Wi-Fi when possible, saving you money.

✔ **Forget This Network:** If you've accidentally logged onto an unwanted network, choose this to forget the network. That stops Windows from logging on again automatically when you're within range. (It also lets you start over if you think you've somehow botched the settings.)

✔ **Turn Sharing On or Off:** Described earlier in this chapter, this option lets you toggle sharing, a handy way to either stop or start sharing your files and devices with other people on the network.

✔ **View Connection Properties:** This switches to the Desktop app's Wireless Network Properties window to change advanced settings.

To see if your Surface recognizes a networked printer, follow these steps:

1. **Open the Charms bar by sliding your finger inward from the screen's right edge.**

2. **Tap the Settings icon; when the Settings pane appears, tap the words Change PC Settings.**

   The PC Settings screen appears.

3. **Tap Devices from the PC Settings screen.**

The PC Settings screen shows every device attached to your printer. They're listed alphabetically, and attached printers have the icon seen in the margin.

Not every Start screen app can print, and there's no way to know if your app is printable until you try. So, open any Start screen app and try to print by following these steps:

1. **From within any app, open the Charms bar by sliding your finger inward from the screen's right edge and then tap the Devices icon.**

The Devices pane appears, listing all the devices capable of working with your app. (Their icons look like the one in the margin.) If you see a printer listed, move to Step 2. No printer listed? Your app isn't able to print, unfortunately.

2. **Tap the desired printer's name, and make any final adjustments.**

The Start screen's Printer window, shown in Figure 6-9, sums up exactly what's going to the printer. It shows a preview and the number of pages required. To see all of the pages you're printing, slide your finger across the preview image from right to left.

To see even more options, tap the More Settings link. There, you can choose the type of printer paper you've using, an essential step when using photo paper on a color printer.

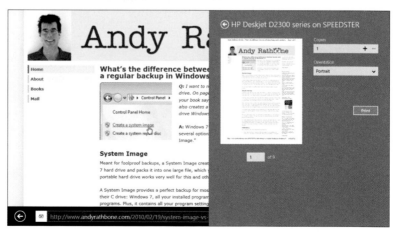

Figure 6-9: The Start screen's Printer window offers minimal adjustments to your print job.

Connecting to a USB hub

Your Surface has only one USB port, and you have many USB accessories. The solution is a USB hub. Similar to a power strip, it plugs into your lone USB hub and offers four or more ports in exchange.

Portable hubs are inexpensive, usually costing less than ten dollars. Choose the smallest, flattest hub you can find so it will lie as flat as possible in your Surface's case. And buy a hub with an attached USB cable. Hubs without cables protrude awkwardly from your Surface's side. If the cable is inadvertently knocked, the force can damage your Surface's lone USB port.

The Windows 8 Pro works with the newer and faster USB 3.0 port hubs rather than the standard USB 2.0 ports used by the Windows RT version. If you own a Surface with Windows 8 Pro, spend a little extra money for a USB hub that supports the faster USB 3.0 speeds.

3. Tap the Print button.

Your Surface sends your information to the printer. But the Start screen's emphasis on speed leaves out some details:

- Many apps can't print. You can't print a day's itinerary from your Calendar app, for example, or even a monthly calendar.

- When printing from the Start screen's Internet Explorer app, you're stuck printing the entire web page — advertisements, comments, and everything in between. There's no way to print selective portions.

- If you need more control over your print jobs on a Surface with Windows 8 Pro, head for the desktop and its cadre of more full-featured programs. Windows RT tablets, unfortunately, don't offer more printer controls on the desktop.

- If your Surface with Windows RT tablet can't print to a networked printer, try plugging the printer directly into your Surface. If the Surface recognizes the printer when plugged in directly, your Surface may also recognize the printer when it's plugged back into the network.

Connecting to Portable Accessories

After you finally sit down at a desk with your Surface, you can plug in a few strategic accessories to give your Surface extra powers. This section describes some gadgets you may want to stuff into your gadget bag; a few well-packed accessories let you transform your Surface into whatever you need, whenever you need it.

If you have a stylus for your Surface, *always* carry it along. The size of a pen, the stylus comes in really handy for tapping the desktop's buttons, as well as editing text, as I describe in Chapter 5.

Connecting a mouse or keyboard

When you reach for your Surface's Desktop app, you'll probably want to reach for your Surface's click-on keyboard, which I describe in Chapter 5. But if you don't have a Surface keyboard, any mouse and keyboard will do. Mice and keyboards come in two types:

- **Wired:** These plug straight into your USB port. In fact, any desktop PC's mouse or keyboard also works with your Surface.

- **Wireless:** Both Surface tablets include *Bluetooth* — a way of connecting to nearby gadgets without wires. You'll find plenty of Bluetooth mouse and keyboards on the market.

When shopping for a mouse and keyboard for your Surface, keep these tips in mind:

- Because you may want to pack your mouse and keyboard when traveling, look for flat, lightweight models. For example, Microsoft's Arc mouse flattens completely for storage and then curls up into a mouse shape when needed.

- Before buying a mouse or keyboard, try one out in your own hands. They're highly personal items, and only you can tell if it feels right for you.

- Look for a Bluetooth keyboard with dedicated Windows 8 keys, giving you one-key access to your Surface's volume, Charms menu, and other features.

Connecting Bluetooth accessories

When you're running out of room to plug in USB accessories, Bluetooth is your friend. Bluetooth works much like Wi-Fi, but it specializes in connecting gadgets that live just a few feet apart.

You can add both a Bluetooth mouse and Bluetooth keyboard to your Surface, leaving your USB port free for other items.

To add a Bluetooth item to your Surface, follow these steps:

1. **Turn on your Bluetooth device and, if necessary, make it discoverable.**

   Most Bluetooth devices include an off switch to save power. Sometimes turning it on is as simple as flipping an On/Off switch; others sense movement, automatically turning on and off when needed.

   Making a device discoverable makes it available to be detected by a computer, usually for a period of 30 seconds. Some devices automatically become discoverable when turned on. Others make you hold down a button until their light begins blinking.

2. **On your Surface, fetch the Charms bar by sliding your finger inward from the screen's right edge. Tap the Settings icon to fetch the Settings pane and then tap the words Change PC Settings.**

   The Start screen's PC Settings screen appears.

3. **From the Devices category, tap the Add a Device icon.**

   The PC Settings' Devices screen appears, shown in Figure 6-10, listing all of your Surface's recognized devices, whether they're currently plugged in or not. When you tap the Add a Device icon, your computer begins searching for adjacent Bluetooth devices that are in discoverable mode.

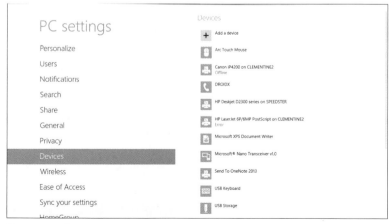

Figure 6-10: The Devices screen lists all of the devices your Surface recognizes. Tap the Add a Device button to add a new device.

If Windows doesn't find and list your device by name, head back to Step 1 and make sure your Bluetooth gadget is still turned on and discoverable. (If it's been longer than 30 seconds, your device may have given up.)

4. **When your Bluetooth device's name appears in the Devices list, tap the device's name so Windows knows to connect to it.**

5. **Type in your device's code, if necessary and, if asked, click the Pair button.**

Everything usually works pretty smoothly until Step 5, where Bluetooth's security measures kick in. Windows needs you to prove that you're controlling both your Surface *and* your Bluetooth device, and that you're not somebody sitting three rows back on the bus trying to break in.

To clear that security hurdle, different Bluetooth devices offer slightly different tactics. Sometimes you need to type a *passcode* — a secret string of numbers into both your device and your computer. (Pull out the device's manual to find the passcode.) Adding to the tension, if you don't type in the passcode quickly enough, both gadgets stop waiting, forcing you to start over.

Some Bluetooth gadgets let you press or hold in a little push button at this step, proving you're holding it in your hand.

After your new gadget successfully pairs with your Surface, its name and icon appear in the Devices category of the PC Settings screen, shown in Figure 6-10.

 To remove a device shown in the Devices list in Figure 6-10, tap its name and then tap the minus sign that appears to the right of its name. Finally, tap the Remove button that appears in the pop-up menu.

Connecting a digital camera and importing your photos

Nobody likes viewing photos on a camera's tiny screen. Thankfully, Windows makes it easy to import your camera's photos onto your Surface, where they shine on the big screen. And you can do it all from the Start screen, making it an easy task to perform while in the field.

Best of all, you needn't install any of the software that came with camera; Windows handles it all.

To import your camera's photos into your Surface, follow these steps:

1. **Turn off your camera and then plug the camera cable's USB plug into your Surface's USB port.**

   Plug the small end of your camera's cable into your camera. The cable's larger end plugs into your Surface's USB port, shown in Figure 6-11, found on the Surface's right side.

Figure 6-11: Plug the large end of your camera's cable into your Surface's USB port, located on the right side.

2. **Turn on your camera and wait for your Surface to recognize it.**

   Wait for a little announcement in your computer screen's top-right corner. The announcement, called a "toast" in some manuals, lists your camera's name and asks you to Tap to Choose What to Do with This Device.

   Tap the announcement, and then move to the next step. (If the announcement disappears before you can tap it, turn your camera off, wait a second, and then turn it on again; the announcement reappears.)

3. **Choose how to import your photos.**

   The next announcement, shown in Figure 6-12, offers several options on how to handle your newly recognized digital camera. These three options always appear:

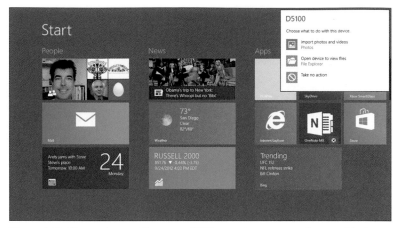

Figure 6-12: Choose Import Photos and Videos to import your photos with the Start screen's Photos app.

- **Import Photos and Videos:** The easiest method, choose this to import your photos with the Start screen's Photos app; move to Step 4.

- **Open Device to View Files:** If you prefer to import your files from the desktop, choose this option. The desktop offers more control, but works better with a mouse and keyboard than your fingers. This option fetches File Explorer (Chapter 12), where you can manually copy the photos from the camera to a folder of your choosing.

- **Take No Action:** This simply cancels the importing process, which is handy if you decide to postpone importing them.

  After you've chosen an option, Windows remembers it, automatically taking the same route the next time you plug in your camera.

4. **When the Photos app appears, choose your options; click or tap the Import button to import your all camera's photos and videos.**

   The Start screen's Photos app, shown in Figure 6-13, tries to keep things simple: It offers to import all your camera's photos and videos into a folder named after the current date. To make a quick and easy transfer, tap the Import button in the screen's bottom-right corner to copy the all the camera's photos and videos onto your Surface. (You can safely unplug your camera from your Surface after importing your photos.)

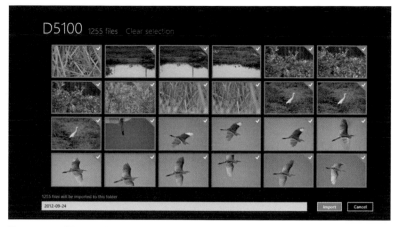

Figure 6-13: Tap the Import button to copy *all* of your camera's photos into your Surface.

But if you don't want to import every photo, or you want to change the name of the folder, you can change those options:

- **Pictures:** The Photos app selects *all* of your camera's photos and videos for importing. To leave behind any blurry ones, tap the ones you *don't* want to import. Or, do you want to import just a few good photos? Tap the words Clear Selection from the screen's top-right corner to deselect all the photos. Then tap just the photos you want to import.

- **Folder name:** To change the incoming folder's name, tap the folder's current name in the white strip along the screen's bottom, shown in Figure 6-13. Then type a different name for the incoming folder.

When you tap the Import button, the Photos app imports your camera's photos and videos. When the Photos app announces that it's finished importing the photos, click the announcement box's Open Album button to see your photos.

The Photos app only imports your camera's photos; it doesn't delete them from the camera. Your camera's own menu offers an option to delete the photos or format its memory card.

Connecting to a Monitor, HDTV, or Digital Projector

The screen on your Surface is larger than an iPad, but it's probably smaller than your desktop PC's monitor. That doesn't mean you've stuck with your Surface's small screen, though. Your Surface includes a high-definition video port that lets you plug in desktop monitors, HDTV sets, and many digital projectors used for PowerPoint presentations.

Because all three of those potential monitors plug in the same way, this section refers to them all as *monitors*.

Plugging in a monitor not only gives you a larger screen, it gives you *two* screens: Your Surface's screen stays active, as well.

This section explains how to connect a monitor to your Surface, as well as tell the monitor to begin displaying your Surface's input. Finally, I explain all four ways your Surface can send its signal to your monitor.

Connecting your Surface to a monitor

In theory, connecting your Surface to a monitor is quite simple: Connect a cable between your Surface's video port and your monitor's input port.

The challenge is finding the *right* cable. No single cable works in every situation. That's because Windows 8 tablets and monitors contain different types of video ports. And your cable needs the correct jack on each end, or it won't fit.

Both Surfaces can connect through HDMI, although both do it in slightly different ways:

- Surface with Windows RT contains a microHDMI port.
- Surface with Windows 8 Pro contains a miniDisplayPort port.

TVs and monitors also include one or more different types of video adapters.

- **HDMI:** Shown in Figure 6-14 (right), this port is the same as the ones found on many computers, but it's *full-size* — more than twice as large. HDMI cables also carry the sound as well as the video, a perk when watching movies on a big screen.

On a Surface with Windows RT, the cable's small microHDMI plug pushes into your Surface's video port (on the left in Figure 6-14); on the other end, the standard HDMI plug pushes into your monitor or TV's HDMI port (on the right).

✓ **DVI:** The next most popular, this appears mostly on PC monitors rather than TVs. For DVI, you need a third-party adapter.

✓ **VGA:** This oldster appeared on monitors for nearly 20 years, so it's still around on a lot of equipment as a last-resort connector. Cables and adapters with VGA connectors often cost more because they need more circuitry to translate between the types of signals flowing through the cable.

Matching your Surface's video port with your monitor's port leaves you with three ways to connect the two:

✓ Buy Microsoft's customized adapters. At $40 apiece, Microsoft's stylish adapters contain the correct jack for your Surface on one end, and a VGA or HDMI port on the other. Buy the adapter you need and then plug in your own standard VGA or HDMI cable.

✓ Buy a cable with the right plug for your Surface on one end and the right plug for your monitor on the other end. This might be your least expensive option for HDMI connections.

✓ If you already have a cable that fits into the video port on either your Surface or your monitor, head to Amazon (www. amazon.com), Newegg (www.newegg.com), or your local electronics store to buy an *adapter* for the cable's other end. For example, an adapter can turn a standard HDMI plug into a microHDMI plug that fits into a Surface with Windows RT.

Figure 6-14: Both ends of the microHDMI cable used to connect a Surface with Windows RT to a monitor.

Depending on the variety of external monitors you plan to connect to your Surface, you may need to collect several types of cables or adapters.

 When shopping for HDMI cables, be aware that the higher-priced ones don't make the video signal any better. The cables either work, or they don't.

Making your monitor recognize your Surface

After you've connected the correct cable between your Surface and the monitor and told the Surface to send its signal to the monitor, you face one last challenge. You must convince the monitor to *recognize* your newly plugged-in Surface.

The solution here works a little differently depending on whether you're connecting your Surface to a HDTV or a PC monitor.

 Make sure your Surface is turned on and set to Duplicate mode, described in the next section, so your Surface sends a constant video signal to your monitor. When you see the Surface's screen on the monitor, you'll know you found the right combination.

- ✔ **HDTV:** On your TV's front panel or handheld remote control, look for a button for switching between video inputs. Keep pressing the remote's Video Input button, switching between inputs, if necessary, and your Surface's screen will eventually appear.

- ✔ **Monitor:** If your monitor is already connected to another PC, unplug the second PC. (You can plug the cable back in when you're through.) Your monitor should sense your Surface's signal and automatically begin displaying it. (Sometimes turning the monitor on and off again helps it switch to the right signal.)

It might take a little fiddling, but you eventually see your Surface appear on the big screen.

Windows's four different ways of using an attached monitor

After you've connected your Surface to a monitor with the right cable, you need to tell your Surface exactly *how* to send its image.

Windows offers you four options, and you can see them by following these steps:

1. **Swipe your finger inward from any screen's right edge to fetch the Charms bar and then tap the Devices icon.**

2. **Tap the Second Screen icon, and choose how your Surface should send its signal.**

   It offers four choices, shown in Figure 6-15:

   - **PC Screen Only:** This recognizes the second monitor, but keeps it blank, only displaying your Surface's screen. It's handy mostly when connecting to a projector at a meeting or conference. You can set up everything on your Surface without everybody having to see your busywork on the projector. Then, when you're ready to wow the crowd, switch to one of the other modes, described next.

   - **Duplicate:** Perhaps the easiest way to use two monitors, this simply duplicates your Surface's screen onto the second monitor or projector. It's great for presentations, and it lets you control what you see on either screen with whatever seems natural at the time. When your fingers touch the Surface, you see the effect on both screens.

   - **Extend:** This extends your Surface's Desktop app across your second monitor, giving you an extra wide desktop. Or, you can keep the Start screen on your Surface, and run the Windows desktop on the larger, second screen.

Figure 6-15: Choose how Windows 8 should handle your newly connected monitor.

• **Second Screen Only:** This blanks the Surface's screen, sending the display only to your second monitor. It's a simple way to connect a larger monitor, but you lose the benefits of your touchscreen tablet. Unless you're trying to mimic a desktop computer, complete with a mouse and keyboard, use the Duplicate feature instead.

After you tap your choice, your Surface may blank its screen as it looks for and connects to the second screen. A moment later, your Surface's screen appears on the second screen.

Working on two different monitors simultaneously may be confusing at first. These tips help you adjust to this strange new configuration:

✔ When setting up the second monitor for the first time, choose Duplicate. That makes it a lot easier to see if your monitor is recognizing your Surface.

✔ Your Surface's sound piggybacks along with its video through both an HDMI and a miniDisplayPort cable. However, the sound plays through the speakers built into your monitor or TV set. If you want better sound, route the HDMI cable to your home stereo, and from there to your HDTV.

✔ When you choose Extend, Windows makes the screen extend off your Surface's right edge and onto the second monitor. To change that, visit the Desktop app's Control Panel. In the Appearance and Personalization category's Adjust Screen Resolution section, you can tell Windows which way to extend the desktop: left, right, up, or down.

✔ That same Adjust Screen Resolution section's Detect and Identify buttons help you figure out which monitor is which and then position the two screens to meet your needs.

✔ If you're accustomed to using a mouse, the mouse-clickable corners on Windows 8's desktop work on both monitors. Point and click in either monitor's lower-left corner to fetch the Start menu, for example.

Adding Portable Storage

Your Surface's drive is speedy but tiny, especially when compared to today's desktop PCs, which usually include more than 300 GB of storage space.

Because apps can be installed only on your Surface' internal drive, that doesn't leave you much space for your own files.

If you need more storage, your Surface offers you several options, each serving different needs:

- **Memory slot:** This slot in your Surface, hidden beneath the kickstand, accepts a tiny memory card that holds 64 GB or more. You can swap memory cards to access different batches of files, but memory cards can be expensive and cumbersome to move around.

- **Portable hard drive:** Essential for people who collect a lot of information in the field, portable hard drives let you tote a huge amount of files. Today's portable hard drives can hold 3 TB of information: That's about *3,000 GB*, which should be more than enough space until you return to your desktop PC.

- **Flash drives:** Flash drives work best for quick file transfers between PCs and your Surface. When you need to copy files onto your Surface, copy them to your flash drive from your PC. Then, insert the flash drive into your USB port and copy the files to your Surface's hard drive. (If you can't find a printer that's compatible with your Surface with Windows RT, copy files to a flash drive, and then print them from your desktop PC.)

The rest of this section describes these storage spaces in more detail. And if that's not enough room, drop by the following section: "Connecting to the Cloud with SkyDrive."

Connecting to built-in memory cards

Your Surface includes a special slot for sliding in a tiny memory card. Many cell phones accept the same type of memory card: microSD, microSDHC, or microSDXC.

To insert a card on a Surface with Windows RT, open your Surface's kickstand to expose the slot, shown in Figure 6-16, and then push the card (letters side out) into the slot until you hear it lock into place. (It will slide out just a bit when locked into place.) Your Surface makes a joyous beeping sound as it recognizes the card. (On a Surface with Windows 8 Pro, push the card into the slot on the Surface's left side.)

To remove a card from either Surface model, push it back into the slot until it unlocks and then pull it out.

Figure 6-16: Push the card into the slot until it locks into place.

I explain how to copy information to and from cards and other storage spaces in Chapter 12.

✔ The microSDHC cards can hold up to 32 GB, whereas the newer microSDXC cards currently come in capacities of 64 GB, with higher capacity microSDXC cards arriving soon.

✔ You can't store apps on the memory card, but you can store the biggest space hogs: videos, music, and photos.

✔ For easy file transfers, buy a memory card reader that accepts micro SDXC cards. Insert your memory card into the reader and copy files onto it with your PC. Then remove the card and insert it into your Surface to enjoy the card's files.

Connecting to portable hard drives

If you own a large music or video collection, your Surface's hard drive won't be large enough. Only one gadget can handle the job: a portable hard drive, like the one shown in Figure 6-17.

Plug the cable from one of these small hard drives into your Surface's USB port. After a few moments, the drive shows up in File Explorer, covered in Chapter 12.

Figure 6-17: Plug a portable hard drive into your tablet to carry huge amounts of files, songs, or videos.

Most portable hard drives draw their power directly from your Surface's USB port. Some older drives won't work because they need more power than your Surface can give.

Portable hard drives typically hold up to 3 TB of information, which is about 3,000 GB. That should be enough to last most people while on the road.

Connecting to flash drives for file transfers

An essential addition to your gadget bag, flash drives are tiny memory sticks that plug into the USB port on your Surface's side. After they're inserted, the drive appears in File Explorer.

Flash drives are the simplest and fastest ways to copy files to or from your Surface. In fact, they're why Windows 8 tablets beat many competing tablets: Few other tablets even include a USB port, much less let you copy files to and from a flash drive.

I explain how to copy files to and from drives in Chapter 12.

Connecting to the Cloud with SkyDrive

Today, it seems every company wants you to save your files on the *cloud*. That's technospeak for an *online storage place to stash your files*. Microsoft, Amazon, Google, and a host of other companies offer free Internet storage spaces for you to store your files.

All Surface tablets include an app to access Microsoft's brand of cloud, called *SkyDrive*. Depending on when you signed up, SkyDrive offers you from 7 to 25 GB of space for you to stash your files. After you fill up that space, Microsoft offers you two choices:

- ✔ Delete some old files to make room for your newer, incoming files.
- ✔ Pay up. For a larger space, Microsoft charges a yearly fee that increases as your storage space grows.

SkyDrive offers many advantages, especially for a storage-starved Surface. After you stash files on SkyDrive, you can access them from *any* Internet-connected tablet, computer, or phone.

You can access your SkyDrive-stashed files several different ways: from your Start screen's SkyDrive app, the Windows desktop's SkyDrive folder, or even through a web browser at http://www.skydrive.live.com. And, if you lose your Surface, your SkyDrive files stay safe and password-protected in the cloud.

Now, the odd parts about SkyDrive. The Start screen's SkyDrive app lets you view, open, and download your SkyDrive files. It even lets you upload files. But it won't let you upload *folders*, making it awkward for mass operations. And when you're setting up SkyDrive for the first time, you usually want to stuff it full of files you need while traveling.

So, to stock your SkyDrive more quickly, install Microsoft's SkyDrive for Windows program on your *desktop*, described in the next section.

The Windows RT version of Surface can only run the SkyDrive app; you can't install the SkyDrive program on its desktop. However, the RT version's SkyDrive app can still upload and download files from SkyDrive, covered later in the "Managing files with the SkyDrive app" section. And if you install SkyDrive for Windows on your desktop PC, you can easily share files with your Windows RT Surface.

Installing SkyDrive for Windows and uploading files to SkyDrive

For the easiest access to SkyDrive, install Microsoft's SkyDrive for Windows program on your Surface with Windows 8 Pro tablet *and* your desktop PC.

To keep things simple, SkyDrive for Windows places a handy SkyDrive folder in the Navigation pane of every folder on your Windows desktop.

Anytime you add folders or files to your computer's SkyDrive folder, SkyDrive automatically synchronizes them with your SkyDrive space on the Internet. That makes those files available to *all* of your computers, tablets, and phones.

To download and install the desktop's SkyDrive for Windows program and begin stocking your SkyDrive account with files, follow these steps:

1. **From the Windows desktop, download and install SkyDrive for Windows.**

   Open Internet Explorer on the Windows desktop and then visit the SkyDrive for Windows website (`http://windows.microsoft.com/skydrive`). Follow the instructions to download and install SkyDrive for Windows onto your Surface with Windows 8 Pro tablet, as well as your desktop PC.

   That same web site also offers apps for your Android, Apple, and Windows phones, so they can access your SkyDrive-stored files, as well.

   Tablets with Windows RT can't install SkyDrive for Windows on the desktop. Instead, install SkyDrive For Windows on your home PC and then move to Step 2.

2. **Decide whether to make your PC or tablet's files available to other devices and then tap the Done button.**

   SkyDrive's installation program tosses you an odd question before closing: Make Files on this PC Available to Me on My Other Devices?

   The answer to this question takes some serious thought, so I cover it in the sidebar, "Turning your desktop computer into a cloud." For now, though, deselect the check box before tapping or clicking the Done button. (You can turn it back on later.)

3. **When asked, sign in with your Microsoft account.**

   As SkyDrive finishes installing on your desktop, it asks you to sign in with your Microsoft account. Here, you type in the same e-mail address and password you use when signing onto your Surface with a Microsoft account.

4. **Open the SkyDrive folder.**

   When you finish downloading, installing, and signing into SkyDrive, the program places a SkyDrive folder in the Navigation pane of every folder on your desktop, shown in Figure 6-18.

5. **Copy files and folders to SkyDrive folder.**

   The SkyDrive folder works like any other folder on your PC. You can drag and drop folders and files into it. Or you can copy and paste files into the SkyDrive folder. (I describe how to copy and move files and folders in Chapter 5.)

Feel free to add files you might need while on the road: favorite photos, for example, favorite music, and backups of important files.

Managing files with the SkyDrive app

After you've stocked SkyDrive with files, you can access those files quickly and easily from your Surface with the SkyDrive app. If you can't find the app, download it for free from the Windows Store, which I cover in Chapter 7.

The SkyDrive folder in the Navigation pane

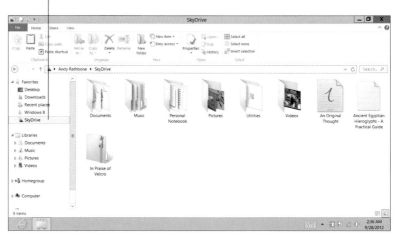

Figure 6-18: SkyDrive for Windows places a SkyDrive folder in every folder's Navigation pane that automatically synchronizes with the web's SkyDrive.

When you want to upload or download files using the SkyDrive app, follow these steps:

1. **From the Start screen, tap the SkyDrive app.**

   The SkyDrive app fills the screen, shown in Figure 6-19, showing all of your folders and files uploaded to your SkyDrive account. Although they're the same folders and files shown in Figure 6-19, the app shows them in a slightly different style.

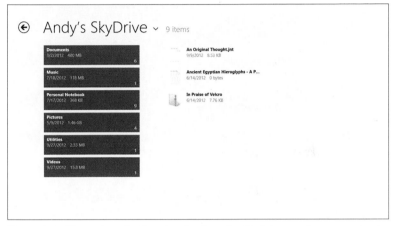

Figure 6-19: Shown here in Thumbnails view, the SkyDrive app lets you upload or download files on your SkyDrive storage space.

   If it the SkyDrive app doesn't show your files, make sure you're connected to the Internet. You can't connect to SkyDrive without it.

2. **Tap what you'd like to open.**

   Tap a folder, and it opens to display the files and folders inside.

   Tap a file, and a program or app opens it. If a file *doesn't* open, you don't have a program or app on your Surface that's capable of opening it.

3. **To upload new files, fetch the App menu bar and tap the Upload icon.**

   To fetch any app's App menu bar, slide your finger up from the screen's bottom edge.

Turning your desktop computer into a cloud

When you finish installing SkyDrive for Windows on your desktop, the program leaves you looking at a check box next to this odd sentence: *Make your PC or tablet's files available to other devices.*

If you deselect the check box, the program simply installs SkyDrive For Windows, letting you stock your SkyDrive storage space with files and folders.

If you leave the check box selected, however, Windows adds something extra to SkyDrive: It lets you access *that entire PC* from the SkyDrive web site. That's right: All of your PC's files, folders, libraries, and drives will be available through SkyDrive. And because it takes place from the website, Surface with Windows RT owners can browse their desktop PC's files from the Internet, as well.

Leaving that check mark in place automatically expands your Surface's storage space to include *your entire desktop PC.* Naturally, Microsoft took some security precautions with such a bold move. Before letting you access a new PC for the first time, SkyDrive asks you to type in a code.

In the background, Microsoft sends a text message to the cell phone or e-mail associated with your Microsoft account. When you receive the message, you type it into the computer you're using to access the PC. When Microsoft receives the matching code, it adds that PC to your list of accessible PCs.

You can only access PCs you've left turned on, so you'll need to leave your desktop PC turned on to access it from the road. If you're planning on using this handy SkyDrive feature, be sure to enter your cell phone number when setting up your Microsoft account.

The File Picker appears, described in Chapter 4, ready for you to select the file or files you'd like to upload. (The SkyDrive app lets you upload only *files*, not folders.)

You can select several files within a folder by sliding your finger downward on their tiles. To select them all, tap the words Select All along the top of the File Picker.

Fetching SkyDrive's App menu bar in Step 3 reveals more than just the Upload icon. The App menu bar also offers these options:

 ✔ **Refresh:** Tap this to tell SkyDrive to refresh its list of files and folders, which is handy if you're waiting for something uploaded from another computer.

 ✔ **New Folder:** This creates a new folder in SkyDrive, an essential task when organizing files.

✓ **Upload:** Covered in this section, this lets you choose files to store on SkyDrive.

✓ **Details/Thumbnails:** This switches SkyDrive from Thumbnail view (shown earlier in Figure 6-19) to Details view, which lets you fit more information on the screen.

✓ **Select All:** This selects everything on the screen — files and folders. After they're selected, you can tap either of the two new icons that appear: Clear and Delete. (You probably won't use this much.)

Chapter 7

All About Apps

- -

In This Chapter

▶ Making the most of Windows 8's bundled apps

▶ Customizing apps to meet your needs

▶ Updating out-of-date apps

▶ Downloading new apps

▶ Uninstalling or changing apps

▶ Installing and uninstalling desktop programs

- -

*W*indows 8 brings many changes, but one of the most baffling is that it no longer likes the word *program*. For example, programs – software that runs on the Windows desktop – are now called *apps* in the world of Windows 8. Confusingly, Windows 8 uses the term *apps* for programs running on the Start screen, as well.

This odd nomenclature confuses things. For example, the Windows RT version can run *only* Start screen apps. The Surface with Windows 8 Pro, by contrast, can run both apps *and* desktop programs. Microsoft simply says they both run *apps*, as if the word *programs* no longer exists.

It's way too early to retire the word "program," as it still appears on all your old software boxes, installation discs, and manuals, so this book refers to Windows desktop software as *programs*.

Mini-programs that run on the Start screen are called *apps*.

With that bit of linguistics taken care of, this chapter tackles a more important topic: Just what can you *do* with the darn things on your Surface?

Mini cheat sheet for apps

The Start screen serves up a smorgasbord of apps, each built to handle a specific task. But no matter how much the apps differ, every app shares the same basic commands. These tips work in *every* app, whether they came bundled with your Surface, or you downloaded them from the Windows Store:

- **Open an app:** From the Start screen, tap the app's tile with a finger. (You can return to the Start screen with a press of your Surface's Windows key.)

- **Close an app:** Apps needn't be closed, as I explain in Chapter 4. But if you *really* want to close your currently viewed app, slide your finger all the down the Surface's screen, from the top edge to bottom edge.

- **Change an app's settings:** Fetch the Charms bar by sliding your finger inward from the screen's right edge. Then tap the Charms bar's Settings icon.

- **Search an app's contents:** Fetch the Charms bar, tap the bar's Search icon, and type your search term in the Search box.

- **Print from an app:** Fetch the Charms bar, tap the bar's Device's icon, and tap your printer's name. (Not all apps can print.)

- **View an app's menus:** Slide your finger up a bit from screen's bottom edge or down a bit from the top edge.

- **Return to your last-used app:** Slide your finger inward from the screen's left edge; your last-used app drags itself into view.

- **See currently running apps:** Slide your finger in slightly from the screen's left edge, and then back to the left edge. A strip appears along the left edge, displaying thumbnails of your currently running apps. To return to an apps, tap its thumbnail.

Making the Most of Apps

You can download and install new apps, covered later in this chapter, but your Surface comes with more than a dozen built-in apps. Most of them live right on the Start screen for easy access.

Others aren't listed on the Start screen, but hide in the Start screen's All apps area. To see *all* of your installed apps, slide your finger up from the bottom of the Start screen and tap the All Apps icon.

But whether they're listed on your Start screen or hiding in the All Apps area, the following apps appear on every Surface tablet:

- **Bing:** You can search for websites directly from Internet Explorer, but Microsoft's Bing search engine app brings a more finger-friendly interface, with its larger buttons, handy autocomplete of search terms, and easy access to trending items.

- **Calendar:** This handy app lets you enter your upcoming appointments, of course. But it can also automatically fetch appointments you've made in online calendars created through accounts with Google or Microsoft. The app then blends appointments from several sources into one calendar. I cover the Calendar app in Chapter 9.

- **Camera:** Your Surface's front camera works best for vanity shots, whereas the back camera is more suited for scenic vistas, if you don't mind looking dorky while holding up your tablet to frame the wonders of nature. I explain how to use your Surface's camera in Chapter 10.

- **Desktop:** A tap of the Start screen's Desktop tile fetches the traditional Windows desktop, covered in Chapter 12. There, you find several of Windows' usual accessories like Paint and Notepad. The Desktop app lets you run all of your old, traditional Windows programs. (Windows RT tablets include the Desktop app, but they can't install your older Windows software.)

- **Finance:** In the U.S., this tile shows a 30-minute delay of the Dow, NASDAQ, and S&P. (In other markets, it shows other indexes.) Tap the tile to open the Finance app, filled with charts, indices, news, rates, and stocks you've added to your personalized Watchlist.

- **Games:** A tap of the Games app brings the Xbox Games app, a link to your Xbox game console. Here, you can see your Xbox friends and gaming achievements, as well as watch game trailers and buy new Xbox games. (The app also lists a few free games to play on your Surface.)

- **Internet Explorer:** I cover this stripped-down version of Internet Explorer in Chapter 8. This no-nonsense browser site fills the screen with your currently viewed website, with no messy menus or tabs to get in the way. (To see the app's menus, slide your finger up from the screen's bottom edge.)

- **Mail:** Described in Chapter 9, this simple app lets you send and receive files and e-mail. It works in conjunction with your People app, automatically filling in e-mail addresses as you begin typing in a person's name.

✔ **Maps:** The Maps app brings up a version of Microsoft Bing Maps. Because neither Surface includes a *Global Positioning System* (GPS) chip, the Maps won't find your exact location or offer turn-by-turn navigation. Instead, it finds your approximate location, and it still dishes up accurate directions when you type in two addresses.

✔ **Messaging:** This universal instant message program, covered in Chapter 9, lets you swap text messages to friends through Facebook, Microsoft's Instant Messenger, and other instant messaging programs.

✔ **Music:** This music player, covered in Chapter 11, plays music stored on your Surface or stashed away on SkyDrive (Chapter 6). But it's also a gateway to Xbox Live Music, which offers an array of streaming music options to owners of an Xbox game console.

✔ **News:** Drop by here to read news pulled from a wide variety of news sources, which differ depending on your region.

✔ **People:** The People app, covered in Chapter 9, contains your friends' contact information. You can enter or edit the details yourself, or let the app automatically harvest your friend's information from your Facebook, Twitter, Google, or other online networks.

✔ **Photos:** The Photos app, covered in Chapter 10, lets you show off your photos, whether they're stored on your Surface, or on accounts from Facebook, Flickr, SkyDrive, or even other Windows computers on your network. It can also import photos from your digital camera.

✔ **Reader:** Many downloadable documents and manuals come stored in Adobe's *Portable Document Format* (PDF), and this app opens them for easy reading.

✔ **SkyDrive:** This app lets you stash files online. It not only lets you share files with other computers and people, but it's a convenient way to add storage to a space-deprived Surface. I cover SkyDrive and other storage solutions in Chapter 6.

✔ **Sports:** Sports fans drop by here to see the latest team scores and game news. Open the App bar and tap Favorite Teams to create a mini-newspaper devoted to your favorite team's news and statistics.

✔ **Store:** To download new apps, visit the Windows Store, covered later in this chapter.

Travel: Designed around people who keep their suitcase packed, this app caters to impulse buyers. It's filled with tempting panoramic photos of travel hotspots, maps, reviews, and, of course, links for booking flights and hotels.

Video: This plays videos from your Surface and its storage areas, as well as providing a portal to Xbox Video, covered in Chapter 10.

Weather: This personalized weather station grants you a weeklong glimpse into your city's future weather patterns. (Load the App bar and tap Places to add other cities to your crystal ball.)

I explain the mechanics of the Start screen in Chapter 4, including tips on adding, removing, and organizing apps on the Start screen.

Customizing apps to meet your needs

Microsoft's built-in apps come preset to cater to the widest audience. But once they're living on *your* Surface, take some time to make them cater to your own needs, instead. Tell the Weather app to display your own city, for example; add your favorite newspapers to the News app, and add your favorite sports teams to the Sports app.

The customization tricks described here apply to most apps, whether they came bundled with Windows 8 or you downloaded them from the Windows Store app.

To customize an app, follow these steps:

1. **Fetch the App menu, called the *App bar*, by sliding your finger up slightly from the screen's bottom, or down slightly from the screen's top.**

   Different apps treat their App bar differently. Some place their menu along the bottom, others drop them down from the top. Some do both.

2. **When the App bar appears, tap its buttons to customize the app to your needs.**

   Fetch the App bar in the News app, for example, shown in Figure 7-1, and the top App bar offers three options:

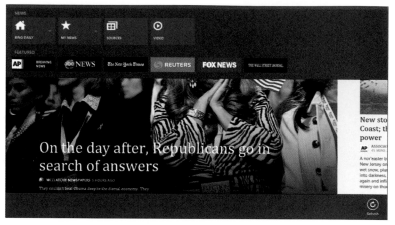

Figure 7-1: To customize an app, swipe your finger up from the screen's bottom or down from the top edge to fetch that particular app's App bar.

- **Bing Daily:** The equivalent of a browser's Home button, a tap of this button returns you to the News app's front page. (It's called Bing Daily because Microsoft's search engine, Bing, constantly stocks the News app with the latest news.)

- **My News:** Tap here to personalize your news with topics of interest to you. To start, tap the plus sign within the Add a New Section box; when the Add a Section screen appears, type in a favorite topic. Tap the Add button, and the My News section collects stories on that topic. Revisit here to see the latest news about that specific subject.

Place quotes around your search term to find results that contain that exact phrase. For example, type **"brussels sprouts"** to see news only about today's trendy vegetable. Type **brussels sprouts**, by contrast, and the app fetches news about Belgium and salad toppings.

- **Sources:** Want to read information from one favorite source? Tap the Sources option to read news from a particular new outlet, including the *New York Times*, *USA Today*, *Time*, Fox News, and the major networks.

After customizing the News app to meet your own interests, try these other tips to personalize your Surface's other apps:

✓ Traveling to a new city? Prepare yourself by opening the Travel app, fetching the Charms bar with an inward swipe from the screen's right edge, and tapping the Search icon. Type your destination into the Search bar, and tap the Search icon. When the travel guide shows your destination, swipe up from the screen's bottom edge and tap Pin to Start; that places a travel guide to that city on your Start screen.

✓ Add your stock portfolio to the Finance app by fetching its App bar, tapping the Watchlist button, and tapping the plus sign to add stocks symbols. After you've added your portfolio, tap any of the stock's symbols to see detailed information about the stock's historical value.

✓ If you click the Allow button when the Weather app first asks your location, the app automatically updates its Start screen tile with your city's weather forecast. To add other cities, fetch the App bar, tap Places, and tap the plus sign button next to those cities' names.

✓ If you don't see any way to customize your app on its App bar, fetch the Charms bar and tap the Settings icon. When the Settings pane appears, check the list near the top edge. Some options let you change or personalize your app's behavior.

Sharing apps with other accounts

If you buy an app, you can install that app on up to five devices, or share it with up to four other people. For example, an app you purchase on your Surface can also be used on your desktop PC, as well as three other computers.

Or, on your Surface, you can share your purchased app with up to four other account holders. To do that, follow these steps:

1. **Have the other account holder log on and visit the Store app.**

2. **In the Store app, switch to your Microsoft account by opening the Charms bar, tapping Settings, and tapping Your Account from the Settings pane.**

3. **Log into the Store with your Microsoft account, tapping Change User, if necessary.**

4. **Find the apps you purchased and install them onto the other user account.**

5. **Revisit the Charms bar's Settings area, tap Your Account, and tap Change User to sign out.**

Repeat this process for each user who wants to use your paid app.

Organizing your apps

Microsoft sets up your Surface's Start screen in a pretty boring way. And as you begin downloading apps, it changes from boring to a sprawling mess that creeps out of sight past the screen's right edge.

To make your Surface *yours*, take control of your Start screen, personalizing it to fit your lifestyle. As I explain in Chapter 4, you can remove tiles for apps you don't use, add tiles for apps you *do* use, move related tiles into groups, and move favorite tiles to front, so they're easy to tap.

After you've done that, Microsoft's Surface will start looking a lot more like *your* Surface.

Downloading new apps from the Windows Store

Your Surface comes with a plenty of built-in apps, described in the previous section. But sooner or later, those won't be enough. When you need to beef up your Surface with more features, there's an app for that: It's called the Windows Store app.

The Store's apps let you mold your Surface around your own interests. Birdwatchers can downloading bird-watching tools. Sailors can download tide-prediction apps. Cooks can download recipe collections.

As programmers write more apps to fill in more niches, Windows 8 keeps growing. And best of all, most of the apps are free.

Because Windows RT tablets can't run desktop programs, they're limited to apps downloaded from the Store app.

To add new apps to your Surface, follow these steps:

1. **Open the Store app.**

   If you're not already on the Start screen, head there with a press of the Windows key. Tap the Store app's tile, and the Store app fills the screen, shown in Figure 7-2.

Updates available

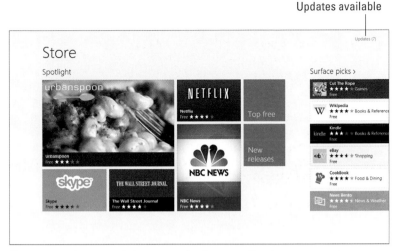

Figure 7-2: In its upper-right corner, the Store app lists how many updates are available for your apps.

If any of your apps have available *updates* — newer versions that add features or fix problems — the store lists them in its upper-right corner. (I cover updates in this chapter's next section.)

The Store app never shows you *all* of its apps. Some apps are limited to people living in certain countries, for example. And Surface with Windows RT owners won't see apps that only run on Windows 8 computers. (Surface with Windows 8 Pro owners see both types of apps.)

2. **Browse for apps, tapping interesting apps to read their description, details, and reviews left by others.**

You can search for a specific app, as I describe in the next step. But if you feel like browsing, the Store app offers several ways to window shop its app collection.

As you browse, watch for the left-pointing arrow in the screen's top-left corner. Tap that arrow to return to the Store page you just left.

To explore the apps, drop by these places in the Store:

- **Top Free:** Be sure to tap the Top Free tile to see the most popular free apps. The quality may surprise you. Each Store category offers its own Top Free tile, which lets you limit your search to a specific category.

- **New Releases:** Although a tap of this tile fetches the latest stuff, it's a mixed bag. There's no filter, so expect to see apps written for other languages or countries. Few shoppers will be interested in an app devoted to another country's railroad timetables, for example.

- **Categories:** As you scroll toward the Store app's right side, the Store's categories appear: Games, Social, Entertainment, Photo, Music & Video, Sports, Books & Reference, News & Weather, Health & Fitness, Find & Dining, Lifestyle, Shopping, Travel, Finance, Productivity, Tools, Security, Business, Education, and Government.

Tap any category's name to browse apps in that category. Some categories offer subcategories. Tap the Games category, for example, shown in Figure 7-3, and you can sort the apps by their game type (adventure or playing card, for example), price, rating, and more.

Figure 7-3: When browsing app categories, tap the drop-down menus along the top to sort the offerings in different ways.

If you spot the app of your dreams, head to Step 4 to install it onto your Surface. If you still can't find the right app, move to the next step and search for it.

3. **Search for an app.**

When you can't find what you want by browsing, try searching. Like every other search in Windows 8, searching for an app begins with a trip to the Charms bar:

Slide your finger inward from the screen's right edge, and tap the Search icon.

When the Search pane appears, type a keyword or two that describes your app in the Search box, then press the keyboard's Search key.

Windows searches the store, shown in Figure 7-4, listing all the matches.

Figure 7-4: Tap the Charms bar's Search icon to search the store by subject.

4. **Tap an app's name to read more about it.**

The app's page in the Store appears, shown in Figure 7-5, offering three ways to see more about the app.

Figure 7-5: Tap the words Overview, Details, and Reviews to find out more about the app.

- **Overview:** The app shows this page by default, shown in Figure 7-5. Here, you see a picture and description of the app, its features, and ways to see more information: The app's website, for example, as well as the app's support page, and legal terms.

Slide your finger across the app's picture to see additional photos. Most apps offer two or more photos of how the app will look on your Surface.

- **Details:** Although boring, this page may be the most important. It elaborates on the details shown in the app's far-right pane, lists what bugs were fixed in the latest release, what processors the app supports, and the permissions it requires.

Windows RT tablets can only install apps written for ARM processors. Windows 8 Pro tablets, by contrast, can only run apps written for x86, x64 processors. (As you browse the apps, the Store only shows apps that run on your particular version of Windows.)

- **Reviews:** The most enlightening part of choosing an app comes from reading the reviews. Here, owners leave comments based on their experience. Judge by the consensus rather than individual reviews: Different people have different expectations.

Looking at an app's pictures, as well as reading an app's Overview, Details, and Reviews pages, lets you know whether the app's right for you or if you should continue browsing.

5. **Install or buy the app.**

When you find an app you want to place on your Surface, the app's page (shown earlier in Figure 7-5) displays any of three buttons:

- **Install:** Found on free apps and purchased-but-uninstalled apps, tap this button to install the program onto your Surface. A minute or so after you tap the Install button, the app appears on the far-right end of your Start screen, ready to launch with a tap of its tile.

- **Try:** Found on paid apps, tap this to try out the app for a week. After a week, the app expires unless you tap the Buy button, opening your wallet for the app's full price.

- **Buy:** Paid apps cost anywhere from $1.49 to $999.99, but most cost less than $5. Tapping the Buy button lets you purchase the app immediately if you've already linked a credit card with your Microsoft account. No credit card link? Then the Buy button takes you to a secure website to enter that information.

  If you don't see a button, the words You Own This App appear, meaning you've already downloaded the app. If it's missing from your Start screen, tap the All Apps button on the Start screen's App bar, as I explain in Chapter 4. That presents an alphabetical list of *all* the apps installed on your Surface.

6. **Wait for the app to download.**

   Most apps download in less than a minute or two. When the app finishes downloading, a notice pops up in the screen's upper-right corner telling you the app was installed.

As the Store's number of apps increases, you'll be able to add many extra powers to your Surface quickly, and easily — a welcome change from the days of old when you needed to slide discs into your computer, hoping everything would work.

When browsing for apps, be sure to tap the Reviews button on the app's page in the Store. That lets you read what other people think of the app, helping you weed out the stinkers.

The Store app is one of the few apps that doesn't *autorotate*: If you hold your Surface in portrait mode, the Store app stays stuck in sideways position. Don't think something's wrong with your Surface. The Store app insists on being held sideways.

Apps constantly change. Companies release newer versions to add features and patch security holes. I explain how to update your apps in Chapter 4.

Apps that run on the Surface with Windows RT are known as ARM apps, named after the Advanced RISC Machines company that created the special low-power chip inside the Windows RT version.

Uninstalling or changing an app

Before you can uninstall or change an app, you need to *select* its tile on the Start screen. Oddly enough, selecting an app's Start screen tile is a task rarely stumbled upon on your own. So, here's the secret:

To select an app on the Start screen, slide the app's tile slightly upward or downward with your finger.

After you select an app, a checkmark appears in the app's top-right corner, like the Travel app shown in Figure 7-6. The App bar also appears along the bottom, listing everything you can do with your newly selected app.

Figure 7-6: After you select an app, the App bar appears along the screen's bottom, letting you choose how to change that app.

✔ To uninstall an app, tap the Uninstall button from the App bar.

✔ App bar icons also let you change the size of an app's tile, start or stop the app's live updates, or unpin (remove) the app from the Start screen.

✔ In Windows 8, you select an item by sliding it in the *opposite* direction it normally moves. Because the Start screen scrolls from right to left, for example, you slide a tile up or down to select it. Use this trick whenever you want to select something in Windows 8 or within any of its apps.

✔ Selecting the Start screen tile of a traditional Windows desktop program brings a slightly different set of icons to the App bar. You can open the program in a new desktop window, pin it to the desktop's taskbar, or view its location in the desktop's File Explorer program.

✔ You can select more than one app at a time, handy when weeding out unwanted tiles to remove from the Start screen.

Installing Desktop Programs

Surface with Windows RT tablets include a traditional Windows desktop, but with one big restriction: They won't let you install any programs onto the desktop. Instead, Surface with Windows RT tablets are limited to downloads from the Windows Store app.

Surface with Windows 8 Pro tablets, by contrast, include a fully functional desktop, just like the one found on desktop PCs. But because tablets don't come with disk drives, how do you install a desktop program?

The Surface with Windows 8 Pro gives you several options:

✔ **Windows Store:** When you browse the Windows Store app with a Windows 8 Pro tablet, many desktop programs appear on the Store's list of apps. When looking at a program you want, tap the Go to Publisher's Website link. The software publisher's website appears, where you can buy the program, if required, and download the program's installation file.

✔ **Website:** Desktop programs not listed in the Windows Store can still be downloaded directly from the Internet, just as in previous versions of Windows.

✔ **Flash drive:** All Surface tablets include a USB port. You can copy or download a program's installation file onto a flash drive with another computer, and then insert the flash drive into your Surface with Windows 8 Pro's USB port and install it from there.

✔ **SkyDrive:** Described in Chapter 6, this online cubby hole works well for swapping files between your Surface and desktop PC. From your desktop PC, copy a program's installation file to any folder in SkyDrive. Then, open the Start screen's SkyDrive app, visit the SkyDrive folder, and tap the program's installation file to install it.

Chapter 8

Browsing the Web

· ·

· ·

*T*he Internet-hungry Windows 8 includes two web browsers. The Start screen's nimble browser works easily with your fingers. The old-school browser on the Desktop app provides extra power, by contrast, but works best with a keyboard and trackpad or mouse.

Although the two browsers behave quite differently, they're oddly intertwined: They share your Home page, logon passwords, browsing history, and your list of favorites sites, among other things. Adding to the confusion, both browsers bear the same name: Internet Explorer.

This chapter covers your tablet's two versions of Internet Explorer. It explains how they work, how they differ, and which one works best in which situations.

Not yet connected to the Internet? Flip back to Chapter 6, where I explain different ways your Surface can connect with the Internet.

Opening the Start Screen's Internet Explorer App

 To open the Start screen's browser, tap its icon (shown in the margin) on the Start screen. The browser opens, filling the screen as shown in Figure 8-1.

Figure 8-1: Like all Start screen apps, the Internet Explorer app hides its menus, filling the screen with your website.

When opened, the Start screen's browser displays one of these three things:

- ✔ **Your home page:** When opened for the first time, the Start screen's browser displays your *home page:* a favorite site you've chosen to display whenever you open Internet Explorer. If you haven't chosen a home page, as I describe later in this chapter, Microsoft fills the screen with one of its own websites.

- ✔ **Your last-visited site.** Unless you specifically *closed* the browser after your last visit, the browser displays the same site you last visited. (I explain how to close apps in Chapter 4.)

- ✔ **You're not connected.** When the browser displays this alarming message, it means your Surface isn't receiving an Internet connection. (I explain how to connect with the Internet in Chapter 6.)

But no matter which page your browser displays upon opening, notice how the page completely fills the screen. That makes the page easier to read, but it also highlights the Internet Explorer app's greatest weakness: The browser hides all of its menus.

You probably won't miss the menus much, though. The browser loads quickly, works very well with your fingers, and you can easily tap one site's links to jump to another site. The fast-loading browser excels at serving up quick bits of information, which is what most people need from the Start screen. If you need more power, head for the desktop version of Internet Explorer, covered later in this chapter.

The rest of this section explains everything you need to know about the Start screens' nimble browser: how to find and open its menus, load websites, jump quickly to favorite sites, simultaneously browse several sites, share and download files and information, and adjust your browser's settings — all with your fingertips.

Open the Start screen browser's menus

Like most Start screen apps, the browser app hides its menus. That lets you concentrate on the picture rather than the frame. When you need the menus, you can reveal them using the same trick that summons the menus from any Start screen app:

Slide your finger inward from the screen's top or bottom edges.

As you slide your finger, it drags the menu into view, snapping it along the screen's top or bottom edges, as shown in Figure 8-2.

Each icon on the App bar performs a different task with a tap of your finger:

✔ **Back arrow:** Tap this to revisit your previously viewed web page.

✔ **Address bar:** To type in a new web address, tap inside the address bar. If no keyboard is attached, the touch keyboard appears, ready for you to type in the address of the website you'd like to visit. (As you type, the area above the address bar lists matching names of previously visited sites. Spot the name of the site you want to visit? Tap its name to load it.)

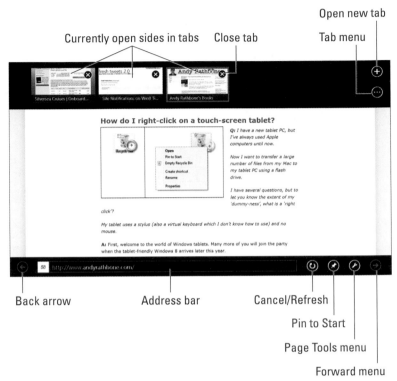

Figure 8-2: To see the browser's menu, called an *App bar*, slide your finger slightly inward from the screen's top or bottom edge.

  ✔ **Cancel/Refresh:** As you view a site, this becomes a Refresh button; tap it to reload the page, retrieving the latest content. This becomes a Cancel button while a web page loads; if the site takes too long to load, tap it to stop trying to load the sluggish site.

  ✔ **Pin to Start:** Tap this to pin the site's name and icon to your Start screen This not only makes for easier launching from the Start screen, but makes it easier to launch from within the browser itself, as I explain in the next section.

  ✔ **Page tools:** When a page doesn't load properly, tap this little wrench icon. When the pop-up menu appears, choose View on the Desktop. That opens the site in the *desktop* version of Internet Explorer. (If the wrench icon sprouts a plus sign, that means that site offers an app for easier access.)

  ✔ **Forward arrow:** After clicking the Back arrow to revisit a site, click the Forward arrow to return to the site you just left.

✔ **Tabbed sites:** Along the top edge, the browser lists thumbnail pictures of other sites currently open in your browser. To revisit one, tap it. To remove one from the list, tap the X in its upper-right corner.

✔ **Open new tab:** A tap of the plus sign icon in the top right lets you open a blank new tab. That lets you open a new web page, handy when you want to compare two websites. (You can jump between the sites by tapping their thumbnails on the top menu.)

✔ **Tab menu:** Dedicated to the tabbed sites shown on the top row, this icon brings a pop-up menu with two options: Close tabs, which closes all the open tabs, and New InPrivate tab, which opens a new tab for browsing in private (covered in the sidebar).

The Start screen browser may look lightweight, but it's actually fairly full-featured, providing everything you need for casual browsing. As shown in Figure 8-2, the browser lets you open several sites simultaneously, each in their own tabs.

I describe how to close the Internet Explorer app in Chapter 4, but there's really no need to close Internet Explorer or any other Start screen app. They're designed to stay open constantly, letting you switch between them as needed, also described in Chapter 4.

Navigating a website with your fingers or mouse

Being designed specifically for your fingers, the Start screen's version of Internet Explorer works quite well with touch controls. When browsing a website, you can easily do any of these tasks with a touch of a finger:

✔ **Scroll through a web page:** When viewing a web page, remember the "sliding a piece of paper" rule: Slide your finger up or down the page, and the web page travels along the screen with your finger. By sliding your finger up or down the page, you can read the entire page, skipping up or down a few paragraphs at your own pace.

✔ **Enlarge tiny text:** When the text is too small to read, place two fingertips on the screen and then spread them. As your fingers move, the information expands, enlarging the text. Pinching the screen between two fingertips shrinks the page. By stretching and pinching, you find the sweet spot for easy visibility of both text and photos. (A quick double-tap makes the page as large as possible, letting you pinch it down to your preferred size.)

✔ **Fetch menus:** Slide your finger up slightly from the screen's bottom, or down slightly from the screen's top. A menu pops up along the screen's top edge, bottom edge, or both.

✔ **Open a link in a new tab:** Hold your finger down on the link until a square appears. Lift your finger, and a pop-up menu appears. Tap Open Link in new Tab. (To access pages open in tabs, slide your finger down slightly from the screen's top edge and then tap the thumbnail of the page you want to revisit.)

TIP

Browsing in private

Most websites leave lasting impressions long after they've left your eyes. Days or months later, the sites' names can still pop up in your address bar as you begin typing a few letters. They linger in your browser's history of visited websites. They often leave behind *cached* photos — copies of viewed photos — on your computer's hard drive. And they leave behind *cookies* — small files that help the website track your visits.

When you want to visit a website without leaving a trace, head for the Start screen browser's InPrivate mode from the Tab menu. InPrivate mode lets you shop for holiday presents, visit controversial websites, or browse on a public computer without letting the next person know your business.

To turn on InPrivate mode on the Start screen's browser, follow these steps:

1. **From the Start screen's Internet Explorer app, slide your finger down slightly from the screen's top edge to reveal the menu.**

2. **Tap the Tab menu (it looks like three dots) and, when the pop-up menu appears, tap New InPrivate tab.**

A blank InPrivate window appears in the browser, ready for you to browse without leaving a trace.

The desktop version of Internet Explorer, covered later in this chapter, requires different steps to enter InPrivate mode:

1. **Tap the browser's Tools icon in its upper-right corner. (The icon resembles a gear.)**

2. **When the drop-down menu appears, tap Safety.**

3. **When the Safety pop-out menu appears, tap InPrivate browsing.**

A new version of Internet Explorer opens, showing a window that says *InPrivate Is On.*

To leave InPrivate mode in either program, just close Internet Explorer, or close the browser's InPrivate window.

The Start screen's Internet Explorer and a trackpad or mouse

Most of the time, you use the Start screen's Internet Explorer with your fingertips. But armed with your Surface keyboard's trackpad or a mouse, the app tosses these new moves your way:

- **Back/Forward:** As you browse between a string of websites, hover your mouse pointer over the current page's left or right edges. An arrow appears along the edge, letting you click to move backward or forward, revisiting previously viewed pages.

- **Opening menus:** To fetch the menus from Internet Explorer and any Start screen app, right-click a blank portion of the web page, away from words and pictures, and the menus appear.

- **Dragging:** As you drag a mouse in Google maps, Google automatically fills in the formerly off-the-edge portions. It's handy, for example, to see what's just north of the currently viewed screen. When you try dragging with a finger, though, Windows thinks you're trying to move the entire screen; it doesn't limit your movements to the map's contents. Moral: Use a mouse if possible when viewing Google Maps.

Visiting websites

You don't always have to open Internet Explorer to begin browsing. If you spot a web link inside a piece of e-mail, for example, tap the link. The Start screen's Internet Explorer app appears automatically to display that website.

Tap a link on a web page, and the browser obligingly opens that link, as well, letting you see its contents. And if you've pinned a favorite site to the Start screen with a tap of the App bar's Pin to Start icon, a quick tap of that site's Start screen tile brings it to the forefront.

The app lets you visit sites in other ways, as well:

- **Return to your last visited site.** Slide a finger up from screen's bottom until a menu appears; tap the left-pointing arrow. (Conversely, a tap on the Forward arrow returns to the site you left.)

🖝 **Type in a site's address.** Slide your finger up the page to fetch the menus, and begin typing the site's name in the address bar, shown earlier in Figure 8-2.

🖝 **Visit a favorite site.** When you tap in the address bar, described in the previous tip, look directly above the address bar. There, Windows lists three categories of sites: Pinned (sites you've pinned to the Start screen), Frequently Visited, and Favorites (sites you've marked as favorites). To scroll through them all, slide your finger from right to left. Tap a site's name to revisit it.

🖝 **Revisit a previously visited site.** As you begin typing a site's name in the address bar, the browser checks your list of favorite sites, listing sites that match what you're typing. If you spot your desired site's name before you finish typing, tap the site's name for a quick revisit.

Windows remembers quite a bit about what you do on Internet Explorer. It remembers every term you've searched for, as well as every site you've visited. Although that sometimes comes in handy when trying to relocate information, some view it as an invasion of privacy. I explain how to tackle Internet Explorer's nosy memory in the sidebar, "Making Internet Explorer forget."

Making Internet Explorer forget

Windows offers two ways to control what your browser remembers about the time you spend online:

🖝 **Delete your search history.** To delete your search history from the Start screen's version of Internet Explorer, fetch the Charms bar and tap Settings. When the Settings pane appears, tap Internet Options. Finally, when the Internet Explorer Settings pane appears, tap the Delete button beneath the words Delete Browsing History.

🖝 **Stop Windows from saving searches.** To tell Windows not to remember items you've searched for, fetch the Charms bar and tap Settings. When the Settings pane appears, tap Change PC Settings from the pane's bottom. When the PC Settings window appears, tap Search from the left pane. Finally, turn off the toggle switch called Let Windows Save My Searches as Future Search Suggestions.

Changes made here also affect the desktop's version of Internet Explorer. That version offers additional privacy controls, covered later in this chapter.

Managing several sites in tabs

It's not obvious, but the Start screen's version of Internet Explorer often keeps several sites open at the same time. For example, you may be viewing a website, and then switch to the Mail app, and tap a link somebody e-mailed you.

The Start screen's Internet Explorer appears, displaying the e-mailed website. What happened to the web page you were viewing previously? The browser places it on a hidden *tab* — a storage place the browser uses to juggle several open sites simultaneously.

You can open websites in different tabs, too, a handy trick when you want to visit a page, but keep the first page open for reference.

To open a link in a new tab, follow this simple step:

Hold down your finger on a link. When a pop-up menu starts to appear, lift your finger. Then, from the pop-up menu, tap Open Link in New Tab, as shown in Figure 8-3.

Figure 8-3: When the pop-up menu appears from a held-down link, tap Open Link in New Tab.

To see your currently open tabs, slide your finger down slightly from the top edge of Internet Explorer app. When the menus appear, the top menu lists all the sites currently open in tabs, as shown in Figure 8-2.

To revisit a site, tap its name; the browser switches to that tab.

After a site lives on a tab, it stays there, even if you restart your computer. In fact, tabbed sites only close if any of these three things happen:

- ✔ You manually close a tabbed site by clicking the X in the thumbnail's upper-right corner.

- ✔ You close the browser manually, usually by swiping your finger from the screen's top edge all the way to the bottom. (The next time you open the browser, only your home page appears.)

- ✔ You open more than eight tabs. The browser only has room for eight tabbed sites. If you open a ninth, your oldest tab disappears to make room for the newcomer.

Making sites available with one tap

Eventually, you'll run across a site you don't want to forget. When that happens, "pin" the site to your Start screen. Seeing that tile on the Start screen jogs your memory that you haven't visited for awhile. And, it lets you remedy that with a tap on the tile.

To pin a site to the Start screen, follow these steps.

1. **While viewing the site, slide your finger up from the screen's bottom to see the app menu.**

   The app menu rises from the screen's bottom, shown earlier in Figure 8-2.

2. **Tap the Pin to Start button.**

   The browser quickly creates a new tile using the website's colors, and then sticks that tile on the Start screen's far right edge. (The tile also bears the website's name.)

When you want to revisit the site, tap its icon from the Start screen. Or, open the browser's bottom menu and tap the address bar; a list of pinned sites appear above the address bar, letting you revisit one with a tap on its name.

The Start screen always tacks new items onto its far right edge. To manage your Start screen's inevitable sprawl, head for Chapter 4, where I describe how to separate the Start screen into organized groups of tiles.

Sharing sites and their information

Eventually, you stumble upon something worth sharing with friends. It may be an entire web page; it may be just a recipe's ingredients and instructions from a cooking site.

In previous Windows versions, you'd probably reach for the age-old copy-and-paste trick to shuttle the information to your friends.

Windows 8 updates that maneuver with the easier-to-use Share icon. Sharing items begins with a trip to the Charms bar:

 Fetch the Charms bar by sliding your finger in from the right edge and then tapping the Share icon, shown in the margin.

When the Share pane appears, shown in Figure 8-4, you see every app capable of sharing your screen's current contents. For example, tap the Mail icon, and the Share pane shows the Mail app, letting you type in an e-mail address and send the page on its way.

Share pane

Apps capable of receiving onscreen information

Recently e-mailed person

Link of current web page

Figure 8-4: Tap the Charms bar's Share icon to see how to share your currently viewed or selected item.

The Share pane shows these items, from top to bottom:

🖊 **Link's name:** The web link you're sending appears at the top.

🖊 **Previous recipients:** The Share pane lists the last five people or apps you've shared things with previously. Tap a listed e-mail address to share the item with that person again, saving you the bother of typing in their e-mail address.

🖊 **Apps capable of sharing:** Here, the program lists all of your apps capable of sharing web links. Tap an app to load the app and share the link.

When you spot the People app listed, as shown in Figure 8-4, tap it to share the web link with your social networks. You can send the link via a Twitter or a Facebook post, for example.

Not all apps can share, and some apps can only share certain things. If you don't see an app listed, it's not able to share that particular content.

Downloading files

The Start screen's Internet Explorer app can download files, just like its full-sized cousin on the desktop. To download a file from a website, tap the website's download button. A permission bar appears along the screen's bottom, shown in Figure 8-5.

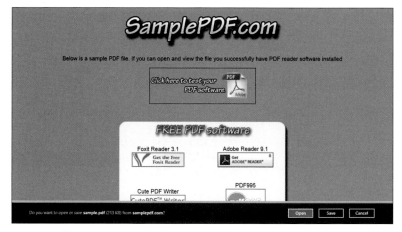

Figure 8-5: From the menu along the site's bottom edge, tap Run to download and run the file, or tap Save to save the file to run later.

Depending on your download, the permission bar offers different options:

✔ **Run:** Tap this option if you're downloading a program to install onto your Surface Pro tablet. The browser downloads the program and then automatically installs it, saving you some time.

✔ **Open:** This downloads and opens the item for viewing.

✔ **Save:** This saves the file in your Downloads folder, handy when you're downloading something you want to access later.

✔ **Cancel:** Tapped a Download button by mistake? A well-placed tap on the Cancel button stops the download.

To find your Downloads folder, open the Desktop app and then open any folder. The Download folder lives in every folder's Navigation pane along the left edge. (Look in the Favorites area.) Tap the Download folder's name to open it.

If you own a Surface with Windows 8 Pro, I explain how to install saved program files in Chapter 12. (Surface with Windows RT tablets can only install programs downloaded from the Store app.)

Changing settings

The Start screen browser, like nearly all apps, lets you tweak its settings to meet your particular needs. And, just as with all apps, opening the settings area begins with a trip to the Charms bar, described in these steps:

1. **Fetch the Charms bar by sliding your finger inward from the screen's right edge. Tap the Settings icon.**

   The Settings pane appears.

2. **Tap the words Internet Options, near the top of the Settings pane.**

   The Internet Explorer Settings pane appears, shown in Figure 8-6. The Internet Explorer app is built for speed rather than power, so it only lets you change these things:

   • **Delete Browsing History:** Don't want anybody to see websites you've browsed? Tap the Delete button to delete them all. (The desktop's Internet Explorer lets you delete specific entries, as I describe later in this chapter.)

   • **Permissions:** Some sites ask for your physical location. The Weather app, for example, wants to send you a *local* forecast. Other apps simply want to target their advertising to your current surroundings. Leave the

Permissions toggle set to On, and the browser politely asks permission before revealing your location to a nosy website. Toggle it off, and all sites automatically know your location. (Tap the Clear button to revoke location permission from sites that have previously had access.)

- **Zoom:** Handy when you can't read the tiny text on websites, this sliding bar lets you choose the magnification level to view sites. If you've set up the desktop to enlarge the screen by 125 percent, as I describe in Chapter 12, this will be set at 125. That's fine for most websites — you can pinch or stretch them to the size that best displays their content.

- **Flip Ahead:** Described in the "Turning on Flip Ahead" sidebar, this lets you read websites like reading a book, flicking the pages from right to left. To turn it on or off, tap the toggle switch. (The word On or Off appears next to the toggle switch, letting you know which way it's switched.)

- **Encoding:** Helpful mainly to bilingual Surface owners, this area lets you change how the browser displays sites containing foreign languages.

3. **Tap anywhere on the web page to close the Internet Explorer settings pane and return to browsing.**

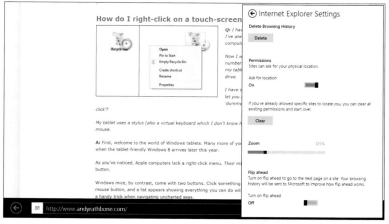

Figure 8-6: To see the menus, slide your finger slightly inward from either the top or bottom menus.

Your changes to the Internet Explorer app's settings take place immediately.

Turning on Flip Ahead

Windows 8's Start screen apps usually move their pages across the screen *horizontally*. That lets you swipe your finger in from right to left to move to the next page, much like you do when reading a book.

Websites, by contrast, expect you to move *down* the page, which is contrary to Windows 8's natural movements.

The solution? Microsoft's new Flip Ahead technology purports to fix things. When you turn on Flip Ahead, Microsoft reformats web pages in the background as they flow onto your screen. To scroll down the page, just flip your finger from right to left, just like turning a book's page: The website's next page appears.

Although this makes web browsing more like flipping magazine pages, the cost is a loss of privacy. Turning it on sends Microsoft a link to every web page you visit, which allows them to format the pages in advance. If you're not concerned about privacy, though, it might enhance your web browsing experience.

It can also break the natural flow of some websites, leaving awkward page breaks. To try out Flip Ahead, visit the Internet Explorer app's Settings area, described in the previous section.

Beware, however: The Flip Ahead feature won't work for every site, even when it's turned on.

Sending a site to the desktop's browser

Not all sites display properly in the Start screen's minimalist, finger-friendly browser. Some sites don't show everything, for example; other sites protest with cryptic error messages that leave you with frustration rather than solutions.

Instead of giving up and moving on to another site, try routing the site to the desktop's more powerful browser, which specializes in coddling cranky websites.

To route a misbehaving site to the desktop's web browser, follow these steps:

1. **Swipe your finger up from the screen's bottom to fetch the browser menu.**

2. **From the browser's bottom menu, tap the Settings icon.**

It's a little wrench with a plus sign, shown in the margin.

3. **Choose Send to Desktop.**

The Desktop app appears, Internet Explorer in tow. Internet Explorer's savvier tools usually help the site display its wares to its fullest capacity.

If the Settings icon's pop-up menu offers the words Get App for this Site, tap that, instead. That takes you to the Windows Store, where you can download an app that accesses the site, translating it into a more finger-friendly experience.

The Desktop's Browser

The desktop browser works much like the one in earlier Windows versions. In fact, it's almost identical to the one in Windows 7. On your Surface, you may find yourself opening it mostly after you attach a keyboard cover or plugged in a mouse and keyboard. Combine a keyboard with the Desktop app, and you can pretend you're working at a desktop PC.

To open the desktop browser, tap the Start screen's Desktop app and then tap the Internet Explorer icon (shown in the margin) from the taskbar along the desktop's bottom-left edge.

The desktop browser offers many more settings than the Start screen's browser. And because some of those settings also affect your Start screen's browser, you'll find yourself heading there periodically just to change the settings described in the rest of this section.

Setting your home page

The Start screen's browser doesn't offer a way to set a *home page* — the page your browser display shows when first opened. Instead, it merely piggybacks on the home page you set in the desktop's version of Internet Explorer.

So, to set your home page on *both* browsers, load the desktop version of Internet Explorer and follow these steps:

1. **With the desktop version of Internet Explorer, visit the site you'd like both sites to display when first opened.**

Visit your favorite site by typing its address into Internet Explorer or clicking on a link. When you're viewing the site you'd like to see when Internet Explorer opens, move to Step 2.

2. **Click the Tools icon in the program's upper-right corner. (It looks like a gear.)**

3. **When the drop-down menu appears, tap Internet Options.**

4. **When the Internet Options page opens to the General tab, tap the Use Current button.**

That sets your currently viewed page as your home page that both versions of Internet Explorer show when they're opened after being closed.

 ✔ Because both browsers can show several sites simultaneously in separate tabs, you can also open different sites in the desktop version of Internet Explorer. When you tap the Use Current button in Step 4, it adds *all* of those sites to your home page, and they each open every time you open either version of Internet Explorer.

 ✔ To open a new tab in the desktop version of Internet Explorer, hold down your finger on the taskbar's Internet Explorer icon (shown in the margin). When a menu begins to appear, lift your finger. When the pop-up menu appears, tap Open New Menu. A new tab appears, letting you type in a website address you'd like to visit.

Removing unwanted sites from Search History

Both versions of Internet Explorer remember *everything* you search for on the Internet. You can delete your past searches while in the Start screen's browser, but that strips away *everything:* You not only lose your list of visited websites, but your saved passwords, your cookies, and all other temporary files created while browsing.

To prune your past searches more selectively, fire up the desktop's browser and follow these steps:

1. **Open the desktop version of Internet Explorer, and click the Tools icon in the program's upper-right corner. (It looks like a gear.)**

2. **When the drop-down menu appears, tap Internet Options. Then tap the Delete button in the Browsing History section.**

The Delete Browsing History window appears, shown in Figure 8-7, letting you choose exactly what to delete.

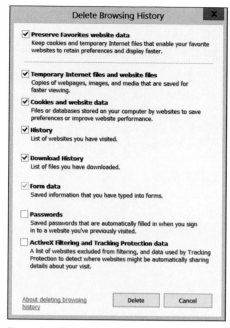

Delete Browsing History ☒

☑ **Preserve Favorites website data**
Keep cookies and temporary Internet files that enable your favorite websites to retain preferences and display faster.

☑ **Temporary Internet files and website files**
Copies of webpages, images, and media that are saved for faster viewing.

☑ **Cookies and website data**
Files or databases stored on your computer by websites to save preferences or improve website performance.

☑ **History**
List of websites you have visited.

☑ **Download History**
List of files you have downloaded.

☑ **Form data**
Saved information that you have typed into forms.

☐ **Passwords**
Saved passwords that are automatically filled in when you sign in to a website you've previously visited.

☐ **ActiveX Filtering and Tracking Protection data**
A list of websites excluded from filtering, and data used by Tracking Protection to detect where websites might be automatically sharing details about your visit.

About deleting browsing history   Delete   Cancel

Figure 8-7: The desktop's Internet Explorer offers much more control over what portions of your browsing history to delete.

3. Tap the Delete button.

The browser deletes what you've chosen, preserving the rest.

For best results, leave the first option checked. That preserves the settings from your favorite sites.

Chapter 9

Reaching Out with Mail, People, Calendar, and Messaging Apps

*N*obody enjoys typing their contacts' names and addresses into Yet Another New Computer. And typing them all in on a glass keyboard makes every Surface owner wish he'd sprung for a Touch keyboard.

Taking mercy on every new Surface owner, Windows 8 *automatically* enters your friends into your contacts list and stashes your upcoming appointments into your calendar. Windows even collects many photos you've posted online, so you can show off all of your photos right from your Surface.

You simply tell your Surface to grab everything from your social networks. Telling Windows about your Facebook, Twitter, LinkedIn, Google, and other accounts lets your Surface automatically harvest your friends' names and contact information. As it searches your social networks for your friends' information, the app also grabs your friends' latest status updates, keeping you up to date.

The end result? When you open your Contacts and Calendar apps, they're already stocked. Yes, after 25 years, computers are finally making some things easier.

Adding Your Social Accounts to Windows 8

Before you can run Windows 8's core apps — Mail, People, Calendar, and Messaging — you need a Microsoft account. (I explain Microsoft accounts in Chapter 3.) Without a Microsoft account, the apps simply display a notice with the words, Sign Up For a Microsoft Account. (Tap those words to sign up for a Microsoft Account on the spot.)

Before the apps can do their job, they need something else, too: your username and password information from Facebook, Google, Twitter, LinkedIn, Hotmail, and other accounts you may use.

Although handing over your password sounds fishy, it's actually safe, secure, and quite convenient on your Surface. Armed with your social networking information, Windows 8 dutifully fills out your Surface's People app with everybody's contact information and stashes your Facebook and Twitter photos in your Surface's Photos app.

To let Windows 8 copy and stash the information that's currently scattered across your social networks, follow these steps:

1. **From the Start screen, open the Mail app.**

   From the Start screen, tap the Mail app's tile, and the Mail app fills the screen, listing any mail you've received from your Microsoft account.

2. **Tell the Mail app about your other accounts.**

   To add your accounts to the Mail app, head for the Charms bar's Settings icon: Summon the Charms bar by swiping your finger inward from the screen's right edge, and tap the Settings icon (shown in the margin).

   When the Settings pane appears, tap the word Accounts, and the Accounts pane appears, listing your Microsoft account. From the Accounts pane, tap the Add an Account link, and the Mail app lists the accounts you can add, shown in Figure 9-1.

Figure 9-1: On its right edge, the Mail app's Add an Account pane lets you enter e-mail accounts from different services.

When you enter the username and password for some mail accounts, the Mail app simply collects any waiting mail. For other mail accounts, like Google, Windows 8 visits a secure area on Google's website where you authorize the transaction.

Repeat these steps for other e-mail accounts you want to add to the Mail app. (Microsoft constantly tinkers with its apps, so don't be surprised to see a few other e-mail accounts listed on your own Surface.)

Don't see your e-mail account listed? I explain how to add missing e-mail accounts in this chapter's sidebar, "Adding other e-mail accounts to Mail."

As of this writing, the Mail app doesn't accept POP mail servers. To add IMAP servers, tap the Other Account option and enter your user name, password, and the name of your IMAP servers.

3. Return to the Start screen, tap the People tile, and enter your other accounts.

When the People app first opens, you may already see a few of your friends, grabbed from online contact lists associated with the e-mail accounts you entered in Step 1.

To stock the app with more of your friends, tell the People app about your social networking sites, like Facebook, Twitter, LinkedIn, and others.

Your importing experience will vary from account to account. For some accounts, you simply need to enter your username and password. Other accounts, like Facebook, take you straight to Facebook's website, where you enter your information to authorize the action, as shown in Figure 9-2.

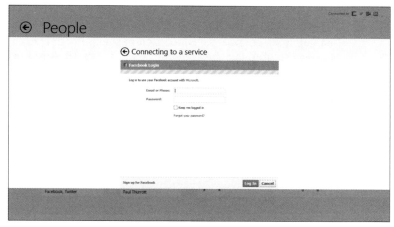

Figure 9-2: Enter your Facebook e-mail account and password to import your friends' names and contact information into your People app.

After you enter your account information, Windows finishes the job, filling your Mail app with e-mail, stocking the People app with your friends' contact information, and adding any appointments to your Calendar app.

- Your contact list updates automatically, constantly reflecting your relationships on Facebook, Twitter, or LinkedIn. If you manually add a contact to one of your online networks from any computer, that person's information automatically appears in your Surface's People app, as well.

- If somebody unfriends you from Facebook, or if you stop following somebody on Twitter, your People app silently erases them without notice.

- In addition to collecting contact information, the People app collects your friends' latest updates from *all* of your social networks. When you visit the People app's What's New section, you can read everyone's updates from every network, without your having to visit them all.

✔ You can still visit the websites of Facebook and other networks to read your friends' updates. The People app simply provides an alternative way to keep track of your friends' lives in a single place.

Sending and Receiving E-Mail

Windows 8's Mail app does a no-frills job of sending and receiving e-mail. It's free, pre-installed, includes a spell checker, and, if you follow the steps in the previous section, it's already filled with the e-mail addresses of your friends.

In fact, you don't even need to open the Mail app to see what's new. The Mail app includes a *live* tile, meaning it constantly updates with the latest information. When you glance at the Start screen, your Mail tile behaves like a mini-billboard, displaying the first few lines of your unread e-mails and their senders' names.

The rest of this section explains how to open the Mail app, send and receive e-mail, switch between folders and accounts, and send and receive files to friends or coworkers.

Adding other e-mail accounts to Mail

The Mail app sends and receives e-mail only from the accounts listed in the Accounts pane described above, which includes e-mail from Hotmail, Google's Gmail, America Online, Outlook.com, and Yahoo!. If you want to read mail from other mail servers, you have two options:

✔ **Read it online:** Launch the Internet Explorer app with a tap of its Start screen tile. Then visit your mail's server's website and read your e-mail online. It bypasses the Mail app, but it's an easy solution.

✔ **Import it to Gmail or Outlook:** In this rather convoluted process, you must set up a *supported* account to import the e-mail from your *unsupported* account. Visit the settings area on Outlook (www.outlook.com), or Gmail (www.google. com/mail). Find the setting where you can import mail from another account. There, enter your e-mail account's username and password. You may also need to enter more complicated information like the site's POP3 and SMTP addresses, found from your mail company's website or technical support staff.

After a supported account imports your other account's e-mail, it routes that account's mail to the Mail app, letting you read everything in one place.

Microsoft eventually plans to support more mail services in its Mail app, sparing you from jumping through these admittedly uncomfortable hoops.

Switching between the Mail app's accounts, folders, and e-mail

A tap on the Mail app's Start screen tile brings the Mail app to the screen, shown in Figure 9-3. Even if the app's already running in the background, a tap on its tile brings it front and center.

Currently viewed account

Currently selected folder   Reply to or forward current e-mail

E-mails in selected folder

Account's   Delete
folders   Write   current
     Contents of selected e-mail   new e-mail   e-mail

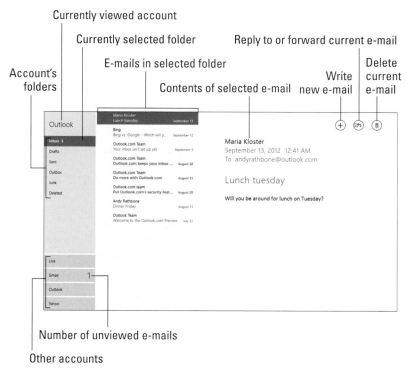

Number of unviewed e-mails

Other accounts

Figure 9-3: The Mail app separates your e-mail into three columns, with your currently selected e-mail spilling out along the right edge.

The Mail app splits the screen into three columns:

- **Left column:** The name of your currently viewed e-mail account appears in the top; that account's folders appear below its name. (You're currently viewing the highlighted folder.) At the column's bottom, you see names of any other e-mail accounts you've set up. To view mail from another account's mail, tap that account's name.

- **Middle column:** Tap a folder from the left column, and a list of that folder's e-mails appears in the middle column. There, you see the sender's name, the e-mail's arrival date, and the subject name.

✔ **Right column:** Tap an e-mail listed in the middle column, and its contents spill out in the right column.

To browse your mail, follow these two steps:

1. **From the left column, tap the account and then the folder you want to browse.**

   When you tap the folder, its contents appear in the middle column.

2. **From the middle column, tap the e-mail you want to read.**

   The message's contents spill out into the right column.

Can't read an e-mail's tiny letters? Then put two fingers on the screen to stretch or pinch it until it's the right size for your eyes.

Figure 9-3, for example, shows an Outlook account in the left column. Beneath it, you see other available accounts, including one from Windows Live, Google's Gmail, Outlook, and Yahoo!. (If you only set up one account, you see only one account listed.)

Mail accounts from different accounts often include different folders. If you've set up customized folders in Gmail, for example, those same customized folders appear in the Mail app. But every account always contains these basic folders:

✔ **Inbox:** When you open the Mail app or switch between accounts, you always see the contents of your *Inbox* — the holding tank for newly received messages. The Mail app only shows your last two weeks of messages; I show how to change that time frame in this chapter's sidebar, "Changing an Account's Settings."

✔ **Drafts:** Started a heartfelt e-mail but can't finish it through your tears? Store it in the Drafts folder to finish later: Tap the Close icon shown in the margin; when the drop-down menu appears, tap Save Draft. Later, when you want to finish the e-mail, tap this folder to see it waiting for completion. (I cover sending e-mail in the next section.)

✔ **Sent Items:** Previously sent e-mail lives in here, letting you reference it later.

✔ **Junk:** The Mail app drops suspected junk mail into this folder. Although the app's Junk filter works well, occasionally visit here to salvage any mistakenly junked e-mail. (Some Yahoo! accounts call this a Bulk Mail folder.)

✔ **Deleted:** Deleted something by mistake? Look in here to find it. To delete something permanently from the Deleted Items folder, select it and tap the Delete icon.

✔ **Outbox:** The Mail app immediately tries to connect to the Internet and send your message. If your Internet connection isn't working correctly, your message lounges comfortably in this folder. After you've connected with the Internet, tap the Sync button, if necessary, to send it on its way.

Like all apps, the Mail app hides its menus. And, like all apps, you reveal those menus by sliding your finger upward from the screen's bottom. The App bar appears, shown in Figure 9-4, with all the app's menus in tow. The App bar is *context-sensitive,* meaning it changes to show icons relevant to what you're currently viewing.

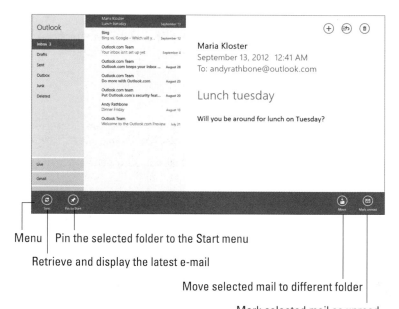

Menu | Pin the selected folder to the Start menu

Retrieve and display the latest e-mail

Move selected mail to different folder

Mark selected mail as unread

Figure 9-4: Slide your finger up from the screen's bottom edge to reveal the Mail app's menu.

Composing and sending an e-mail

To write, spellcheck, and send an e-mail from your Surface's Mail app to a friend's Inbox, follow these steps:

1. **From the Start screen, tap the Mail app's tile and then tap the New icon in the program's top-right corner.**

   An empty New Message window appears, ready for you to fill with your words of glory. If you've set up several e-mail accounts in the Mail app, your e-mail will be sent from the account you last viewed.

Changing an account's settings

Most e-mail accounts let you change how they handle your mail. For example, most accounts contain hundreds if not thousands of e-mails. That's a *lot* of e-mail to sort through. To keep things simple, the Mail app only displays your last two weeks' worth of both sent and received e-mail.

To change that time frame — or to change the settings of any mail account — open the Mail app and follow these steps:

1. **Fetch the Charms bar by sliding your finger in from the screen's right edge, and then tap the Settings icon.**

2. **When the Settings pane appears, tap Accounts; when the Accounts pane lists your e-mail accounts, tap the account you'd like to change.**

   The settings for your chosen account appear, ready for you to make your changes. (To bring more of the Settings pane into view, slide your finger up or down the screen.)

3. **Tap in the area you'd like to change and then change the setting by tapping the adjacent toggle switch, tapping an item from a menu, or typing in words.**

   Your changes take place immediately; you don't need to tap a Save button. To remove accounts you no longer use, tap the Remove account button at the bottom of the account's Settings pane.

To close the Accounts pane, tap anywhere within the Mail app.

To send e-mail from a different account, tap the downward-pointing arrow next to your e-mail address in the screen's upper-left corner. When the menu drops down, tap the name of the account you want to use for sending that particular mail.

2. **Add your friend's e-mail address into the To box.**

   Tap the plus sign to the right of the To box. The People app appears, letting you tap the name of everybody you want to receive the e-mail. Tap the Add button, and the Mail app automatically fills in everybody's e-mail address — a very handy thing on a tablet.

   Or, you can tap inside the To box and begin typing in the recipient's name or e-mail address. With each letter you type, the Mail app scans the contacts listed in your People app, constantly placing potential matches below the To box. If the app happens to guess the right name, tap the name to place it in the To box.

3. Tap inside the Subject box and type in a subject.

Tap the words Add a Subject along the message's top; those words quickly vanish as you type in your own subject, shown at the top of Figure 9-5.

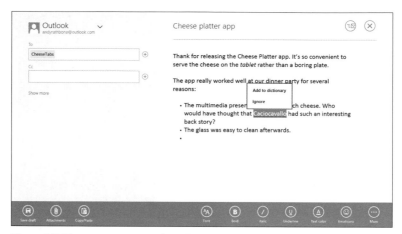

Figure 9-5: Type your message, keeping a watchful eye for any spelling errors caught by the built-in spellchecker.

4. Type your message into the large box beneath the Subject line.

Head to Chapter 5 for typing tips for both the Surface's Type and Touch keyboards, as well as the Surface's built-in keyboard. The Mail app watches as you type, automatically underlining words it doesn't recognize. To correct a misspelled word, tap the underlined word. A pop-up menu appears, shown in Figure 9-5, letting you choose the correct spelling. (Choose Add to Dictionary to add an unrecognized word.)

To embellish your prose, change the text's formatting by swiping your finger upward from the screen's bottom to fetch the App bar. Shown in Figure 9-5, the App bar lets you change fonts, add italics, create numbered lists, and add other flourishes by tapping the appropriate icon.

To save an e-mail in progress, tap the Save Draft button in the App bar's far left. The Mail app saves your e-mail in the Drafts folder of the account you're using to send the e-mail.

5. Attach any files or photos to your e-mail, if desired.

I devote a section, "Sending and receiving files through e-mail," later in this chapter, but here's a starter: Tap the Attachments icon on the Mail app's App bar.

6. **Tap the Send button, located in the screen's top-right corner.**

   The Mail app slides your e-mail through the Internet's blend of fiber-optics and copper wires into your friend's mailbox. Depending on the speed of your Internet connection, mail can arrive anywhere from within a few seconds to a few hours, with a minute or two being the average.

   If you find yourself at a loss for words, tap the Close button, shown in the margin. A drop-down menu appears, letting you tap Delete to delete the message. Or, tap Save Draft, and the Mail app stashes your unfinished e-mail into your current account's Drafts folder for later polishing.

Reading an e-mail

Every time your Surface finds itself connected with the Internet, it automatically grabs any new e-mails it can find. Proud of its background work, the Mail app's Start screen tile updates itself, listing the sender, subject, and first line of your latest few e-mails.

To respond to a particularly enticing e-mail, follow these steps:

1. **Tap the Start screen's Mail tile.**

   The Mail app appears, displaying the first e-mail in your last-viewed account's Inbox, shown in Figure 9-3. Below that, older e-mails appear, listed chronologically.

2. **Open a message by tapping its name.**

   The message's contents fill the window's right edge.

3. **Tap an option from the buttons along the e-mail's top edge:**

   - **Do nothing:** If the message doesn't warrant a response, move on to something more interesting by tapping a different message from the Mail app's middle column.

   - **Respond:** To reply to a message, tap the Respond button in the screen's top-right corner. When the menu drops down, tap Reply. A new e-mail appears, pre-addressed with the recipient's name and subject and containing the original message for you both to reference.

   - **Reply All:** When an e-mail arrives that's been addressed to several people, tap the Respond button, but choose Reply All from the drop-down menu. That sends your response to everybody who received the original e-mail.

- **Forward:** Tap Forward from the Respond button's drop-down menu to sent a copy of your friend's must-see cute cat photo to your own friends.

- **Delete:** A tap of the Delete button moves the message to your Deleted folder. To permanently delete a message, tap the Deleted folder, tap the unwanted message, and tap the Delete button. The message, having no place left to hide, vanishes.

You can print a message the same way you print from any other app: Open the message, fetch the Charms bar, tap the Devices icon, tap your printer from the list of devices, and tap the Print button.

Even though the Map app gathers your e-mail, you can still view your e-mail from your mail service's website in Internet Explorer. Your same e-mails still appear in Gmail (`www.google.com/gmail`), for example, or Hotmail (`www.hotmail.com`).

Sending and receiving files through e-mail

Files, referred to as *attachments* by computer linguists, can be tucked inside an e-mail message. You can send or receive nearly any file, but with a few stipulations:

- Most mail servers can't handle files totaling more than 25MB. That's enough for a song or two, a handful of digital photos, and most documents. That's usually *not* enough to send videos, though.

- If you send a file you've created in Microsoft Word and the recipients don't have Microsoft Word, they won't be able to open or edit your Word file. To avoid confusion, let the recipient know what program you used to create your file.

With those two stipulations out of the way, plunge onward into this section, which explains how to open, save, and send attachments.

Viewing or saving a received attachment

To conserve your precious storage space, the Mail app doesn't automatically download attached files and save them to your Surface. Instead, the Mail app shows attached files using a faintly colored icon, like the one shown in the margin.

Selecting e-mails and moving them to a folder

The Mail app seems incredibly frustrating when it comes to this simple task: How do you select several e-mails and move them to a different folder? But when you know the trick, it's surprisingly easy: To select an e-mail, slide your finger *horizontally* across the e-mail. A check mark appears, showing that the e-mail is selected.

Select as many e-mails in a column as you wish. When you select more than one, the Mail app's menu appears automatically along the bottom. Tap the Move icon, select a destination folder, and you're through.

Whether you want to open or save the attachment, follow these steps:

1. **Tap the word Download next to the attached file.**

   Tap the word Download, and the Mail app to downloads the file onto your Surface. After the Mail app finishes downloading the file, its icon regains its healthy coloring, shown in the margin.

   If you just want to view the attached file (or play an attached song), tap the file's icon and choose Open from the drop-down menu. If your Surface has an app or program capable of opening the file, the file opens, letting you see or listen to the attachment.

   After you've seen or heard the file, you may be done and ready for different adventures.

   But if you want to access it later, give the attached file a more permanent home by moving to Step 2.

2. **Tap the attached file's icon and tap Save from the drop-down menu.**

   Windows's File Picker appears, shown in Figure 9-6. Covered in Chapter 4, the File Picker serves as the Start screen's equivalent of the desktop's File Explorer: It lets you shuttle files from one location to another.

3. **Choose a folder to receive the saved file.**

   Tap the word Files in the File Picker's top-left corner and then choose which library to receive the incoming file: Documents, Pictures, Music, or Videos.

Figure 9-6: To save a file sent through e-mail, tap Files, select a location to save the file, and then tap the Save button.

Don't know where to put it? Choose the Documents library, which serves as a catch-all for anything that's not a photo, song, or movie.

4. Tap the Save button in the File Picker's bottom-right corner.

After you've chosen the file's destination, the File Picker places a copy of the e-mailed file in that location.

5. Repeat these steps to save any other attached files.

Unfortunately, the Mail app doesn't allow you to select multiple files and save them in the same place. So, you must repeat these steps for every attached file you want to save.

Windows 8's built-in virus checker, Windows Defender, automatically scans your incoming e-mail for viruses, worms, and other malware on both Surface models.

✔ Even after you save the file to a folder, it remains in your e-mail. If you somehow lose your saved file, head back to original e-mail and repeat these steps to save a fresh copy.

✔ You can only download attached files when connected to the Internet. That's why it's important to save files you may need to access in areas without Wi-Fi coverage.

✔ To avoid hogging space on your Surface, many e-mail accounts only display your last *two weeks'* worth of messages in the Mail app. After two weeks, those files scroll off your Surface's Mail app.

✏ If you need an attachment you received *three weeks* ago, it might not be lost forever, even if it's scrolled off the Mail app. Try visiting your e-mail's website. Some sites like Gmail let you access all your e-mails, no matter how old they are.

Sending a file as an attachment

Sending a file through the Mail app works just the opposite of saving an attached file, covered in the previous section: Instead of finding a file in an e-mail and saving it into a folder or library, you're finding a file in a folder or library and saving it in an e-mail.

To send a file to somebody through the Mail app, follow these steps:

1. **Open the Mail app and create a new e-mail, as described earlier in this chapter's "Composing and sending an e-mail" section.**

   Choose the recipient and write your message.

2. **Open the Mail app's App bar, and tap the Attachments icon.**

   Open the App bar by sliding your finger up from the screen's bottom edge. (You can do this even if your Surface's on-screen keyboard fills the screen's bottom half.)

   Tap the Attachment icon from the App bar, and the Windows 8 File Picker window appears, shown earlier in Figure 9-6.

3. **Navigate to the file you'd like to send.**

   Tap the word Files to see a drop-down menu listing your computer's major storage areas. Most files live in your Documents, Pictures, Music and Videos libraries.

   Tap any folder's name to see a list of the files stored inside. Don't see the files you want? Tap the File Picker's Go Up link to retreat from that folder and try again with a different folder.

4. **Tap the name of each file you want to send and then tap the Attach button.**

   A tap selects a file; tap a file again to deselect it. As you tap files, their color changes to show they're selected.

   A tap of the Attach button returns to the Mail app and attaches the file or files to your e-mail.

5. In the Mail app, Tap the Send button.

The Mail app sends your mail and its attached file or files to the recipient. Depending on the size of your attached files, this may take from several seconds to several minutes. Because it all takes place in the background, feel free to switch to another app, browse the web, or grab another bagel at your free Wi-Fi spot.

When your recipient receives your attached files, they can save them onto their own computer, no matter what type of computer or e-mail program they own.

- If you try to attach too many large files, the Mail app warns you with a message across the mail's top: "The attachments might be too large to send this message. Try selecting Send Using SkyDrive instead."

- If you spot that message, tap Send Using SkyDrive Instead. The Mail app then uploads those files to a new folder on your SkyDrive account and then sends the recipient a link to that folder where they can view or download them.

TIP

I can't find an e-mail!

Instead of envelopes piling up on a table, e-mail now piles up in your Inbox. And, if you've set up several e-mail accounts, mail can be hiding in several different Inboxes. You can relocate a wayward e-mail with the same tactic used to find things in any Windows 8 app: Summon the Search pane.

From within Windows Mail, tap the account holding the e-mail you want to search for and then slide your finger inward from the screen's right edge. When the Charms bar appears, tap the Search icon.

When the Search pane appears, type in a word you recall seeing in your lost e-mail — even the person's name will do — and then tap the Search key; the Mail app fetches a list of e-mail containing that specific word.

At the time of this writing, the Mail app doesn't provide a way to search through all your accounts simultaneously. To search through *all* of your e-mail accounts, you must use the Search command on each individual account.

Managing Your Contacts in the People App

I explain in this chapter's first section how to link the People app with your online social networks. Your People app then stocks itself with your favorite people, whether they're on Facebook, Twitter, LinkedIn, or other networks.

Open your People app with a tap on its Start screen tile, and the People app appears, shown in Figure 9-7, listing every friend grabbed from your online social networks. And, in keeping with the latest computing trend, People alphabetizes your contacts by their first names. Your friend Adam Zachman *finally* appears first.

Return to the last viewed contact   Edit an account's settings

Avaiable for instant messaging   View your contacts

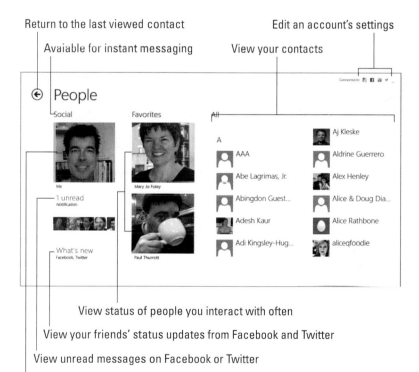

View status of people you interact with often

View your friends' status updates from Facebook and Twitter

View unread messages on Facebook or Twitter

Access your account photo or profile, write updates, or view photo posted online.

Figure 9-7: Tapping in different places on the People app lets you keep up with your contacts, including those pulled in from Facebook, Twitter, and other online address books.

The People app updates itself automatically, adding and dropping people as they enter or leave your social networks.

However, people who don't share their lives through a social network stay out reach of the People app. Also, networks like Facebook contain huge switchboxes full of privacy controls. Some of your friends may have flipped a Facebook switch that keeps their information sequestered in Facebook's walled garden, and away from the clutches of the People app.

The point? You eventually need to remove your gloves and manually add or edit entries in the People app. This section explains the details of a job that can't be sloughed off to the People app's robot crawler.

- ✔ Tapping your way through the People app can lead you to friends, their adventures, and even the adventures of your friends' friends. If you're feeling lost in a sea of people, slide your finger up from the screen's bottom edge and tap the Home button. That takes you back to the front page.

- ✔ When a contact is available to receive an instant message, a thin green bar appears along their picture's left edge. To make yourself *Invisible* — unavailable for instant messaging — open the Messaging app and change your status to Invisible, a task described in this chapter's last section.

Adding contacts

When somebody doesn't appear in your People app, you can add them in either of two ways:

- ✔ Using any computer, add the missing people to the contacts list of one of your online accounts, like Gmail (`www.google.com/gmail`), Hotmail (`www.hotmail.com`), or Outlook (`www.outlook.com/`). Befriending them on Facebook does the trick, too, as does following them on Twitter. After a person appears in a social network or one of your linked online contacts lists, the People app automatically pulls that person's details into your Surface.

- ✔ Manually type your contact's information into the People app. This isn't a one-way street, either; the People app adds your hand-typed information to the online account of your choice, too.

To add a new contact to the People app, follow these steps:

1. **Tap the Start screen's People tile to load the People app.**

   When the People app appears, make sure you're on the home page: Slide your finger up from the screen's bottom edge and tap the Home icon.

2. **Slide your finger up slightly from the screen's bottom edge to fetch the App bar. Then tap the New icon.**

   A blank New Contact form appears, ready for you to type in contact's details.

3. **Fill out the New Contact form.**

   Shown in Figure 9-8, type in your contact's details, including name, address, e-mail, and phone. To add other information, tap the Other Info button. There, you can add tidbits like a job title, website, significant other, or notes that don't fit anywhere else.

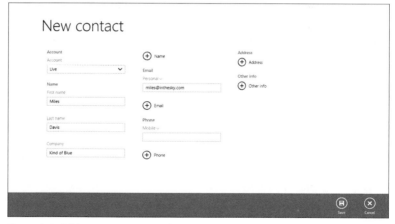

New contact

Account	Name	Address
Account		
Live	Email	Other Info
	Personal	
Name	miles@inthesky.com	
First name		
Miles	Email	
Last name	Phone	
Davis	Mobile	
Company		
Kind of Blue	Phone	

Figure 9-8: Add your new contact's name, as well as any other details you have on hand. Then tap the Save button to add the person to your People app.

Did you add more than one online account into your People app? Then a tap on the Account field in the top left corner lets you choose which online account should also be updated with the new contact. (To update your phone's contacts, choose the account associated with your phone, either Android or Microsoft.)

4. **Tap the Save button.**

The People app saves your new contact, both on your Surface and on the account you choose in Step 3. Spot a typo? In the next section, I explain how to edit an existing contact.

Deleting or editing contacts

As our social and professional relationships change, the People app automatically takes care of the paperwork. When somebody unfriends you on Facebook, they simply drift off your People app without notice. Similarly, if you stop following somebody on Twitter, the People app trims them off your list.

But if you need to edit or delete a contact you've added manually, either on your Surface or on your Google or Microsoft accounts, it's fairly easy to do by following these steps:

1. **Tap the People tile on the Start screen.**

   The People app appears, as shown earlier in Figure 9-7.

2. **Tap the contact that needs changing.**

   The contact's page appears full-screen.

3. **Slide your finger up slightly from the screen's bottom edge to fetch the App bar.**

   The App bar appears as an icon-filled strip along the screen's bottom.

4. **Tap the Delete button to delete the contact; tap the Edit button to update a contact's information. Then tap the Save button to save your editing changes.**

   Tapping Delete removes the person and all his information. No Delete button? That means the People app pulled in his information from a social network. To remove him from the People app, you must first delete him from your social network.

   Tapping the Edit button returns you to the screen shown earlier in Figure 9-8. There, you can update or add information. Finished? Tap the Save button to save your changes.

You can send e-mail from within the People app by tapping a person's name. When her contact information appears, tap the Send E-mail button. The Mail app appears, bearing a pre-addressed New Message window, ready for you to type your message and tap Send. (This trick works only if you have that contact's e-mail address.)

If the People app imported contacts from your Facebook or Twitter accounts, you can't delete any of their imported contact information. But you can *add* information to their contacts page.

Managing Appointments in Calendar

If you manage your appointments on Google's online Calendar or one of Microsoft's accounts, you're in luck: Windows 8's Calendar app harvests that information automatically, just like the People app. The Calendar app also picks up any birthdays it finds on Facebook.

Then it neatly packages all the past, present, and future activity into the Calendar app, shown in Figure 9-9.

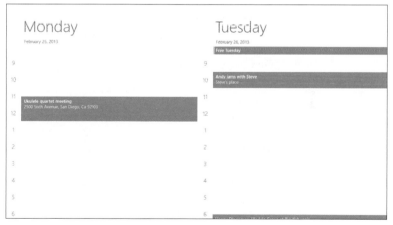

Figure 9-9: Shown here in Day view, the Calendar app stocks itself with your appointments, both those you entered yourself and those from your online social networks.

Don't keep your appointments online? Then you need to add them by hand. And even if your appointments *are* online, you occasionally need to edit old entries, add new ones, or delete ones that conflict with new engagements. This section explains how to keep your appointments up to date.

To add an appointment to your Calendar app, follow these steps:

1. **Tap the Calendar tile on the Start screen.**

   The Calendar appears, shown earlier in Figure 9-9.

2. **Open the Apps bar and tap the New icon.**

   Slide your finger up from the screen's bottom edge to reveal the App bar and its icons, including the New icon for creating new appointments.

3. **Fill out the Details form.**

   Shown in Figure 9-10, most of the choices are pretty easy to figure out: Enter the date, time, duration, location and a *message* — notes about what to bring to the potluck.

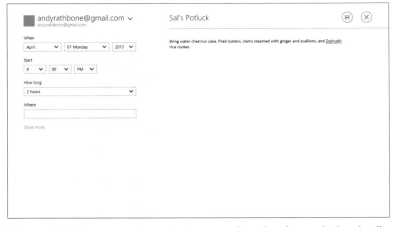

Figure 9-10: Add your appointment's date, start time, duration, and other details.

The Calendar app sends your appointment to your online calendar, as well, if you have one. To see your options, tap the downward-pointing arrow next to Calendar in the top right. A menu appears, letting you choose which online calendar should receive the appointment.

Android phone owners should choose their Google account, so their appointment also appears on their phone. Windows Phone owners, of course, should choose their Microsoft account.

Microsoft's apps don't coordinate well with Apple's online products. But Apple people all own iPads, anyway.

4. **Tap the Save button.**

The Calendar app adds your new appointment to your Surface's Calendar, as well as to the calendar of the online account you chose in Step 3.

When browsing the Calendar app, these tips help you find your way around:

✏ When in use, the Calendar opens to show the view it last displayed, be it day, week, or month. To switch to other views, slide your finger up from the screen's bottom edge to fetch the App bar. Then, tap one of the buttons: Day, Week, or Month (shown in the margin).

✏ To delete an appointment, open it from the Calendar. Then tap the Delete button (shown in the margin) in the appointment's upper-right corner.

✏ To edit an appointment, open it with a tap on its entry in the Calendar app. Make your changes and then save your edits with a tap on the Save icon.

✏ When browsing the Calendar app, flip through the appointments by flipping your finger across the calendar as if you were paging through a book. Slide your finger toward the left to move forward in time; slide it to the right to move backward.

✏ To jump immediately to the current date, slide your finger up from the bottom to fetch the App bar and then tap Today.

Sending Messages with the Messaging App

True to its name, instant messaging programs let you swap messages with friends almost *instantly*. A tap of the Enter key, and your carefully crafted sentence flies across the Internet and onto your friend's screen. Your friend replies, returning the volley with another tap of the Enter key.

Windows 8's friendly Messaging app lets you type back and forth with any contact listed in your People app. It even handles the mechanics of facilitating inter-program banter: Your friend could be typing into Facebook's instant messaging window while you're typing back in the Messaging app's window.

To type messages back and forth to an online friend, follow these steps:

1. **From the Start screen, tap the Messaging tile.**

   The Messaging app fills the screen, shown in Figure 9-11.

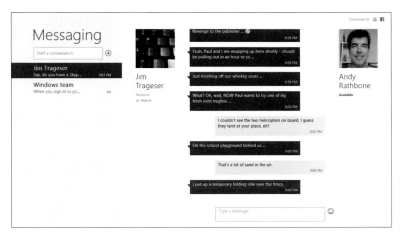

Figure 9-11: The Messaging app, shown with its menus, lists your previous conversations along its left edge. Tap a conversation to revisit its contents.

2. **Tap the plus sign to the right of the Start a Conversation box.**

   Shown in the top-left corner of Figure 9-11, the plus sign fetches the People app's Online mode, which lists only friends who are currently online and available for chatting. If a friend doesn't appear here, he's either not online, not available for chatting, or not listed in your People app.

3. **Tap the name of the person you'd like to chat with.**

   When the messaging window appears, begin typing, as shown in Figure 9-12. Your friend's own messaging system, whether it's on Facebook, a cell phone, or a different system, loads, letting them know you're ready to starting to chat with them.

4. **Type your message, and then press the Enter key.**

   As you type, feel free to edit your message. Your message isn't sent until you press the Enter key. When you press Enter, your message appears in your friend's messaging program. When both finish chatting, simply stop typing, and move onto something else.

Figure 9-12: Press Enter to send your message to your friend.

Even when closed, the Messaging app keep an archive of your conversation. And, when you two chat again, the archive grows longer.

And that brings us to these tips regarding instant messaging etiquette and technique:

✔ To delete a conversation, tap it; it becomes highlighted. Slide your finger up from the bottom of the Messaging app to fetch the App bar. Then tap the Delete icon, shown in the margin.

✔ Don't want to be bothered for awhile? Tap the App bar's Status icon, shown in the margin, and choose Invisible from the pop-up menu. That keeps you from showing up as available in your friends' messaging programs. To reappear to your circle of friends, tap the Status icon and choose Online from the pop-up menu.

✔ Don't be too eager to type. Conversations flow best if you wait for a response before sending another message. Flurries of quick messages make for a disjointed conversation, like a debate full of interruptions.

✔ To monitor who's online and ready to chat, open the People app and slide your finger up from the bottom to unveil the App bar. Tap the Online Only button (shown in the margin) to see friends available for chatting.

✔ Extended chats on a virtual glass keyboard can be difficult because the keyboard covers half of the screen. Switching to a USB, Bluetooth, or Surface keyboard lets your sparkling wit shine through that much more easily.

✔ At the time of this writing, the Messaging app works only
with MSN and Facebook's messaging services. But Microsoft
updates its apps regularly, so don't be surprised to see other
messaging services added.

Chapter 10

Photos and Movies

*Y*our Surface tablet includes two cameras, one on the front and the other on the back. Taking photos with a tablet rarely satisfies, though. There's no viewfinder, and reflections tend to obscure the subject on the screen. Forget about flash or zooming in.

As for quality, your ever-present smartphone probably takes better pictures. Shooting pictures with a Surface just feels awkward compared with shooting through a phone or camera. No, the Surface shines when *displaying* photos and videos, and this chapter walks you through doing both.

Note: Need to import photos from your digital camera or cell phone? I explain how in Chapter 6.

Snapping Photos or Videos

Your Surface displays photos much better than it can capture them. But if you're struck with a Kodak moment and your Surface is the only camera you have handy, follow these steps to snap a photo or movie:

1. From the Start menu, tap the Camera app's tile.

The Camera app appears, shown in Figure 10-1, immediately filling the screen with what it sees before its tiny front or rear lens. (Note how the Camera app's light begins glowing next to the lens, letting you know you're on camera.)

Switch between front and rear cameras

Change camera settings

Set time display settings

Switch between camera or video mode

Figure 10-1: Change your desired controls from the App bar and then touch any other part of the screen to snap the photo.

Folding back the Surface's Touch or Type covers blocks the bottom half of the rear camera's lens. Remove the keyboard cover before snapping a photo.

2. Change controls, if desired.

Contrary to most apps, the Camera app *always* displays its App bar, which offers these options:

- **Change camera:** Tap this to toggle between the front and back cameras. (A light glows next to the camera lens in use.)

- **Camera options:** Rarely used, this button switches the settings from automatic to manual. The limited manual controls rarely work better than the automatic settings.

- **Timer:** Tap this to set a three-second shutter delay, which is *almost* enough time to spring in front of the camera for a group shot.

- **Video/Camera mode:** This toggles between shooting snapshots or videos.

3. To snap a photo or shoot a movie, touch the screen.

When shooting a photo, the Camera app emits a mechanical shutter click sound, and then quickly saves the snapshot. Your new picture quickly scoots out of sight to the screen's left edge, letting you snap another photo.

When shooting videos, a timer appears in the screen's lower-right corner, letting you track your movie's length. To stop shooting the movie, tap the screen.

To view your newly shot photo or movie, slide your finger across the screen from left to right to drag your photo (or the first frame of your movie) back into view. To return to shooting, slide your finger in the other direction, and the live view reappears.

Whether you're looking at a recently shot photo or movie, the Camera app offers a few ways to edit your work, all found on the App bar. Slide your finger up from the screen's bottom to reveal the App bar.

 ✔ **Crop:** Tap this when viewing a photo, and a rectangle appears. Drag the entire rectangle or just its corners to frame a different portion of the photo. Tap OK to crop, and the app saves your crop as a new picture, preserving the original photo.

 ✔ **Trim:** Tap this when viewing a movie, and a circle appears at each end of the video's timeline, shown along the screen's bottom. Drag the circles along the timeline to mark the video's new started and stopping points. Then tap OK to save your video.

Your photos and videos both live in your Picture library's Camera Roll folder, where they can both be viewed with the Photos app, described in the next two sections.

Viewing Photos

The Photos app, just like the People app, makes the rounds of your social networks, picking up any photos it can find. Open the Photos app with a tap of its Start screen tile, and the results appear, shown in Figure 10-2.

The Photos app shows a different tile for each place your photos reside. In Figure 10-2, for example, the first tile contains photos in your Surface's own Pictures library. (The other tiles require an Internet connection for access.)

Figure 10-2: The Photos app shows photos currently on your Surface, as well as online locations like SkyDrive, Facebook, Flickr, and networks.

Follow these steps to view your photos:

1. **Tap the storage area you want to open.**

   To view photos stored directly on your Surface, including ones shot with your Surface's camera, tap Pictures Library. If you have Internet access, tap the other tiles to view photos stored online.

2. **Browse the folders.**

   Tap the Pictures library tile, for example, and the screen shows tiles representing each folder inside that library. Tap a folder to open it.

   To back out of a folder, press the backward-pointing arrow in the top-left corner. Keep pressing the arrow, and you'll eventually return to the Photos app opening menu, shown earlier in Figure 10-2.

3. **Tap a photo to view it full screen.**

   When the photo fills the screen, zoom in or out by pinching or stretching the photo between your fingers. To see its menus, shown in Figure 10-3, slide your finger up from the screen's bottom.

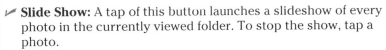

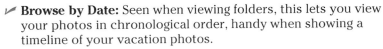

Figure 10-3: The Photos app lets you zoom in and out of photos with your fingertips and watch slide shows.

Depending on whether you're viewing a single photo, a folder's worth of photos, or several folders, the App bar sprouts different buttons:

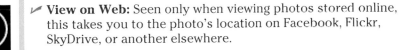

 ✔ **Back Arrow:** A tap of the back arrow in the upper-right corner returns you to the folder containing the currently viewed app.

✔ **Set As:** This brings up a pop-up menu, letting you turn your currently viewed photo into the background for your Surface's Lock Screen, the background for the Pictures app, or the Picture app's tile.

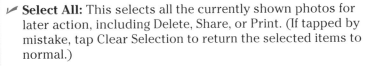 ✔ **View on Web:** Seen only when viewing photos stored online, this takes you to the photo's location on Facebook, Flickr, SkyDrive, or another elsewhere.

 ✔ **Slide Show:** A tap of this button launches a slideshow of every photo in the currently viewed folder. To stop the show, tap a photo.

 ✔ **Select All:** This selects all the currently shown photos for later action, including Delete, Share, or Print. (If tapped by mistake, tap Clear Selection to return the selected items to normal.)

 ✔ **Browse by Date:** Seen when viewing folders, this lets you view your photos in chronological order, handy when showing a timeline of your vacation photos.

Tap the Import button to import photos from an attached camera or your memory card, as I describe in Chapter 6.

When displaying a single photo full-screen, the app bar offers buttons for letting you rotate and crop the image, handy for making profile photos out of group shots.

Sharing or Printing Photos

The Photos app lets you share or print photos by following these steps:

1. **Open the folder containing your photos, and then select the photos you want to share or print.**

   With your finger, swipe down on your desired photos. As you select them with a downward swipe, the selected photos sprout check marks in their upper-right corner.

2. **Visit the Charms bar and choose Share or Devices.**

   Swipe your finger inward from the screen's right edge to fetch the Charms bar, and tap either Share (for sharing with friends) or Devices (for printing your images).

   • **Share:** The Share pane opens, listing every app able to share your photo or video. A tap of the Mail app, for example, opens the Mail pane, where you enter the recipient's e-mail address and tap the Send button. (I cover mailing attached files in Chapter 9.)

   • **Devices:** The Devices pane appears, listing your installed printers. Tap your printer's name, and the Printer window appears, offering you a preview of the printed page. (I cover connecting printers and printing in Chapter 6.)

As more apps appear in the Windows Store, the Share pane offers more ways to share your photos and videos with different social networks. If your social network doesn't yet have an app, visit the site through Internet Explorer to share the photo.

Watching Movies

More a shopping mall than an app, Microsoft designed the Video app to pull you into its two storefronts: The Movies Store entices you buy or rent movies, and the Television Store sets the hook for TV shows. To make sure your wallet's available, you can only use the Video app when logged in with a Microsoft account.

Watching your *own* movies

Movies shot with your Surface's Camera app aren't listed in the Video app. To play them, slide your finger up from the screen's bottom to reveal the Video app's App bar. Tap the Open File icon, and then use the File Picker, covered in Chapter 4, to find your videos in your Pictures library's Camera Roll folder.

The Surface works best with videos encoded in WMV or H.264/MP4 movie formats. If you already own movies in those formats, head for the Desktop app, covered in Chapter 12. There, you can copy your movies to a flash drive, insert the drive into your Surface, and copy the movies to your Surface's Videos library.

The app doesn't support other video formats, like shows recorded by Windows Media Center or TiVo. If your movies are encoded in another format, you need a conversion program to copy them into MP4 format.

To open the Video app and browse its wares, follow these steps:

1. **From the Start screen, tap the Videos tile.**

   The Video app appears, shown in Figure 10-4. The app immediately confuses things by changing its name to *Xbox Videos*. That's because the Video app lets you play videos to your Xbox game console, if you have one, so you can watch your movies on the big screen.

2. **Browse to the type of video you want to watch.**

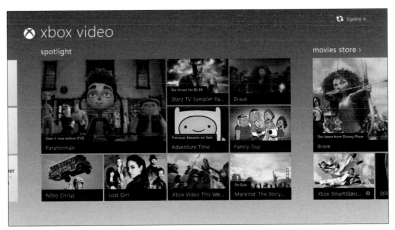

Figure 10-4: The Video app lets you watch your own videos, as well as rent or buy movies and TV shows.

The Video app offers four main sections:

- **My Videos:** Scroll to the hidden area beyond the screen's left edge to see videos living in your Surface's Videos library.

- **Spotlight:** Time-dated offers often appear here, letting you buy movies before they're released to DVD, for example.

- **Movies Store:** Tap any tile to browse trailers, buy, or rent movies.

- **Television Store:** Television shows appear here. (Some shows offer a free episode, usually a season opener.)

3. **Tap a video's tile to see more about it.**

   A window appears, with buttons that let you buy the video, see more about it, watch its trailer or, in the case of TV shows, buy a season package or individual episodes.

4. **Watch a video.**

   Tap a movie or TV show tile from the storefronts to rent, buy, or download the video to your My Videos section. The app charges the credit card associated with your Microsoft account, or prompts you to set one up.

   Tap any video in your My Videos section to begin watching. Swipe up from the screen's bottom to expose buttons for pausing, playing, and skipping forward/backward. The Play To button lets you play the video through your Xbox 360 game console, if you have one.

Before diving into the Video app with your credit card, keep these tips in mind:

- View free things at first to familiarize yourself with the process. Look for free TV pilots, movie trailers, or "behind the scenes" promo videos.

- Rental items and some specials are time-dated, meaning they'll disappear from your Videos library after a certain date.

- Before traveling, look for items with a Download option. After these items are downloaded, they can be viewed when you're out of range of a Wi-Fi connection.

- Before buying anything, you must type in your Microsoft account password, a safeguard against accidentally brushing against a Buy button.

- Don't think you're restricted to your Surface's Video app for movies. Netflix has its own app, letting you watch streaming movies. Amazon's videos are available too, if not in app form, then through your web browser.

Chapter 11

Listening to Music

● ●

In This Chapter

▶ Playing free music through Xbox Music

▶ Signing up for Xbox Music Pass

▶ Playing your own music

▶ Creating playlists

● ●

Some people spend more time organizing their music than listening to it. They store each album in its own folder, meticulously renaming each song's title to include the album name and recording year.

Your Surface, however, isn't built for micromanaging your songs. No, like any tablet, your Surface works best for *playing* music, and the Music app tries to simplify that task.

In fact, you don't even need your own music: Your Surface lets you stream music for free through something called an *Xbox Music Pass*. Or, you can stick to tunes you've copied onto the Surface.

This chapter covers both ways to listen to music: Listening to your own files, or streaming millions of songs from the Internet with Microsoft's new Xbox Music Pass.

Listening to Music through the Xbox Music Pass

When you first open the Music app on a new Surface, you won't find much but an empty shelf. After all, you haven't had time to copy any music onto it yet, a task I describe in Chapter 12.

Even an empty Surface, though, can dish out just about any song you want to hear. Those songs come from an *Xbox Music Pass*, a service Microsoft entices you with when you open the Music app.

If you have no interest in Microsoft's Xbox Music pass, jump to the next section, where you can simply start playing your own tunes.

But if you're curious as to Microsoft's way of letting you listen to more than 30 million songs for free, follow these steps to sample the Xbox Music Pass. (I explain the fine print at this section's end.)

1. **Load the Music app with a tap of its tile on the Start screen.**

   You must sign in with a Microsoft account to hear music through the Xbox Music Pass. The Music app, shown in Figure 11-1, contains four parts:

   • **My Music:** Hidden off to the left, the Music app shows songs or albums you've copied to your Surface.

   • **Now Playing:** Shown when you first open the program, this area lists your currently playing song. Tap any of the surrounding buttons to begin hearing free music.

   • **All Music:** Shown to the right of the Now Playing section, this area lists popular artists and albums, all ready to listen with a tap.

   • **Top Music:** Scroll to the far right to hear something quickly: a list of the latest chart toppers, ready to play with a tap of a finger.

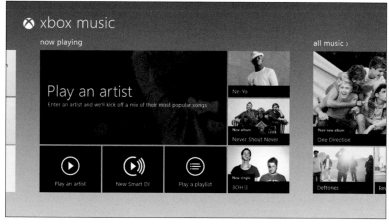

Figure 11-1: The Music app's four sections cater to different interests.

2. **In the Now Playing section, tap the Play an Artist tile, type in your favorite artist's name, and tap the Play button.**

Before the music begins to play, however, you're interrupted by Step 3.

3. **Tap the Sign in Now button to sign up with Xbox, and then tap the I Accept button.**

Microsoft's Windows division and its Xbox division work out of separate offices. So, even though you've signed up with a Microsoft account, you *also* need to sign up for an Xbox profile. (It's free.)

4. **Tap OK to approve the process and listen to music by your chosen artist.**

Your new Xbox profile gives you a nonsensical "gamer tag," which is simply an Xbox nickname. You can safely forget it, as Xbox Music begins greeting you by that name whenever you log on.

After you've dispensed with the red tape, the Music app slips into its Xbox Music clothes and begins playing songs by the artist you chose in Step 2.

You're now free to listen to millions of songs by thousands of artists, simply by tapping the Play an Artist button and typing in the artist's name. Or, tap an artist or album listed in the All Music or Top Music sections listed in in Step 1. It's just waiting to be played.

Now, a moment for the fine print:

- You need an Internet connection to hear the music because that's how Microsoft sends the tunes to your Surface. When you're out of range of a Wi-Fi connection, the music stops streaming.

- Microsoft occasionally slips ads in between songs. Sometimes you just hear a voiceover, at other times, the Music app plays a fullscreen video ad. And after six months, Microsoft limits your ad-supported-but-free streaming to ten hours a month, which is about 20 minutes a day.

- To bypass the ads and the ten-hour monthly limit, sign up for a free 30-day trial. After 30 days, Microsoft begins automatically charging $10 a month to your credit card.

- During that 30-day trial (and if you subscribe to the service), you can play, stream, or download any of the music on your Surface, a Windows Phone, a Windows 8 PC, or an Xbox 360 console (provided you're an Xbox Live Gold member). Those platforms all run Xbox Live, and you can only play the songs through Xbox Live by signing into the service.

✔ If your subscription lapses, you can no longer play your music, including music you've downloaded — *unless* you've bought the music, that is, which costs extra. After they're purchased, however, those individual songs are yours to copy to CD or play on other PCs and music players.

✔ Xbox Music Pass isn't cheap, and it's filled with fine print. But if you pony up $10 a month for the service, it's very convenient — until you stop paying, that is. Then your music disappears, and you're back to ten hours a month of ad-supported music.

Listening to Your Own Music

Whereas the Xbox Music Pass thrives on stipulations, the Music app's other side sets very few rules. You can play music stored on your Surface, its memory card, or on other networked computers. You can even play tunes you've stashed on SkyDrive.

To play your own music on your Surface, follow these steps:

1. **From the Start screen, tap the Music tile.**

   The Music tile opens, shown earlier in Figure 11-1. Eager to push its Xbox Live service, the app places your music out of sight, barely peeking from around the screen's left edge.

2. **Scroll to the screen's farthest left side to see the My Music section.**

   The My Music section lists music stored in your Surface's Music library. If you haven't added any music to your Surface's Music library, the screen looks as empty as the screen in Figure 11-2.

   After you copy music into your Surface's Music library, the screen updates to show up to eight of your albums, as shown in Figure 11-3.

3. **If you spot the album you want to hear, tap it, and then jump to Step 5.**

   If you *don't* see your album, however, tap the words My Music, shown in the top-left corners of Figure 11-2 and 11-3. Your My Music screen appears, shown in Figure 11-4, showing all of your music.

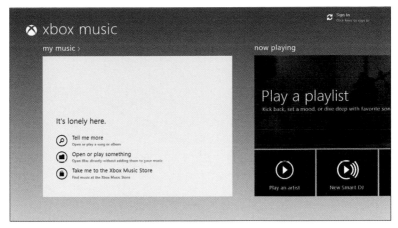

Figure 11-2: If you haven't stored music in your Surface's Music library, the app doesn't show any music.

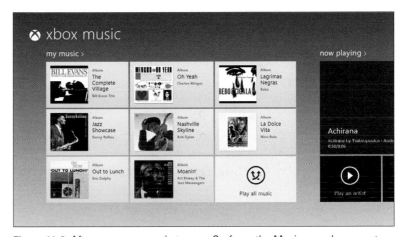

Figure 11-3: After you copy music to your Surface, the Music app shows up to eight of your albums.

4. **Browse through your music by album, song, or artist.**

   Tap the drop-down menu beneath the words My Music in Figure 11-4 to view your music sorted by alphabet, release year, genre, artist, or date added.

   To begin listening to an album or artist, tap its name. A box appears, listing your choice, shown in Figure 11-5.

Figure 11-4: Tap the words My Music, and the Music app shows all of your available music.

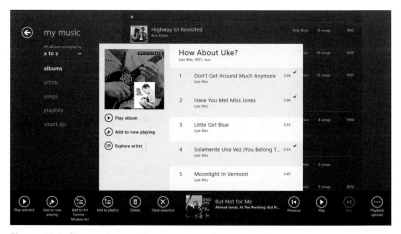

Figure 11-5: Choose how to listen to your chosen music.

5. **Choose whether to play the chosen item, or add it to your Now Playing list.**

   Depending on whether you tapped an album, a song, or an artist, you may see several options in the box shown in Figure 11-5.

   • **Play Album:** This simply begins playing all songs on the album, beginning with the first track.

- **Add to Now Playing:** This tacks the selected item onto the end of your Now Playing list, so it plays after the currently listed music.

- **Explore artist:** Tap this to bring a new window listing more information about the artist, his biography, and his availability on Xbox Music Pass.

- **Play Smart DJ:** Tap this, and the Xbox Music appears, playing a customized radio station built around that artist's style. (And, unless you've paid, you'll hear advertisements, too.)

- **Play all:** This plays all of the songs by the artist you've chosen.

To see more options, slide your finger inward from the screen's bottom or top edge. The App bar appears, shown along the bottom of Figure 11-5, offering different ways to play your music, as well as controls for pausing, fast forwarding, or skipping to the next track on your list of currently playing songs.

 ✔ To create a playlist from the My Music view, select items by sliding your finger horizontally across them; a check mark appears next to selected items. After selecting what you'd like to hear, tap the Add to Playlist button from the App bar along the screen's bottom.

 ✔ You won't hear ads when playing your own music, or music stored on your SkyDrive account. You only hear ads when streaming something from the app's free Xbox Music Pass side.

 ✔ If you hear ads when playing your own music, some Xbox Music streaming files (marked by the icon in the margin) have slipped into your collection. Delete them from your My Music section to stop triggering the ads. Then fetch the Charms bar, tap Settings, tap Preferences, and turn off Xbox Music Cloud.

 ✔ The Surface with Windows RT doesn't include the desktop's Media Player, found in earlier Windows versions. Media Player lives on in the Surface with Windows 8 Pro, however, offering more ways to manage and play your music.

 ✔ The Music app plays only MP3 and WMA files, including WMA lossless. It won't play formats like .flac, .ogg, or .ape.

✔ To hear music stored in places besides your Music library, slide your finger up from the screen's bottom to fetch the App bar. When the App bar appears, tap the Open File icon to fetch the File Picker, covered in Chapter 4. That lets you navigate to the music's location, be it on your memory card, a flash drive, or another networked computer.

 ✔ Your Surface's Touch and Type keyboards have dedicated music playback keys along the top row, right after the Escape key. The first key mutes the sound, the second lowers the volume, the third raises it, and the fourth toggles between play and pause.

Making the Music app concentrate on *your* music

If you prefer listening to your own music, tell the Music app to stop tempting you with the Xbox Music Pass: Follow these steps to make the Music app open with a view of your *own* music library:

1. **From the Music app, open the Charms bar with an inward swipe from the screen's right edge.**

2. **Tap Settings, and tap Preferences from the Settings pane.**

3. **When the Preferences pane appears, turn on the toggle called When the App Opens, Show My Music.**

That tells the Music app to open with a view of your own music, rather than music from Xbox Music Pass's artists of the day.

Chapter 12

Visiting the Windows Desktop

....

....

The Start screen and its apps ecosystem specialize in serving up information while you're on the run. You can find appointments, scan the headlines, check the e-mail, browse the web, listen to music, and still step onto the subway before the doors close. When you sit down, your Surface doubles as an ebook reader, letting you browse books, magazines, and newspapers.

But when you need to *create* rather than consume, your Surface can transform once again: It can mimic a desktop PC, ready to support your own muse or that of your boss. Your Surface's Windows desktop lets you manage files, create documents, and crunch numbers into neatly formed columns.

The Desktop app in your Surface works much like the desktop found in previous Windows versions, so I won't spend much time here with the bare basics. Instead, I walk you through the most common desktop task a Surface owner needs: transferring files onto your Surface so you can access them while on the run.

What's missing from the Surface with Windows RT Desktop?

The Surface with Windows RT offers 8 to 13 hours of battery life, but that life comes at a price: The Windows RT version's Desktop app isn't powerful enough to run traditional desktop programs. The Desktop app still works, however. And Microsoft Office's heavyweights — Microsoft Word, PowerPoint, Excel, and OneNote — wait for you on the desktop.

But you can't install any *other* traditional Windows programs onto the Windows RT version's desktop. Also, these desktop staples, included in Surface with Windows 8 Pro tablets, are missing from Surface RT tablets: WordPad, Windows Media Player, Windows Media Center, Sticky Notes, and Windows Journal.

On the positive side, the Windows RT tablet's desktop still includes File Explorer for managing files, as well as Paint, Notepad, Calculator, and a few other Windows staples.

Making the Desktop Finger-Friendly

Although the Desktop app looks like a normal Windows desktop, don't forget it's just an app. And, as with all other apps, you still have the Charms bar at your disposal, making it easy to jump between apps.

The Charms bar's the only part about the desktop that's finger-friendly, though. The desktop remains rooted in the mouse-pointer-controlled menus of yesteryear.

You can make things easier by telling Windows to make everything on the desktop *larger*. After you flip that switch, everything on your desktop expands.

Following these steps packs less information onto the screen. But you'll at least be able to take advantage of the information you see. And these steps are reversible, letting you return to mouse-sized controls if needed.

To enlarge everything on the desktop so it's easier to touch, follow these steps.

1. **Launch the Desktop app from the Start menu.**

   The traditional Windows desktop fills the screen.

2. **Summon the Charms bar by sliding your finger inward from the screen's right edge, and then tapping the Settings icon.**

3. **From the top of the Settings pane, tap Control Panel.**

   The desktop's Control Panel appears.

4. **On the Control Panel window, tap the Hardware and Sound category, and then tap the Display.**

   The Display window appears, shown in Figure 12-1.

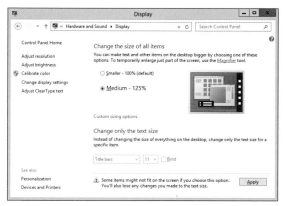

Figure 12-1: Choose Medium - 125% to make the desktop controls easier to touch with a finger.

5. **In the Change the Size of All Items area, tap the setting Medium - 125% and then tap the Apply button.**

6. **When Windows asks you to sign out of your computer and apply your changes, tap the Sign Out Now button.**

   If you haven't saved any work, save it before clicking the Sign Out Now button.

When Windows restarts, your desktop will be larger and easier to control by touch alone.

   ✔ The larger size affects *only* the desktop. Your Start screen and apps remain unaffected.

   ✔ If a crucial portion of an window drops off the screen's bottom, turn your Surface sideways; the desktop automatically rotates, leaving you more space along the desktop's bottom edge. (I explain how to maneuver windows with your fingers later in this chapter.)

~ If you have a stylus for your Surface, don't underestimate its power on the desktop. It works very well as a makeshift mouse, letting you select files and tap buttons, as well as enter and edit text, as I describe in Chapter 5.

Managing Files and Folders by Touch with File Explorer

In earlier versions of Windows, a program named Windows Explorer lets you view your computer's files and storage spaces, shuffling files between them as necessary.

Windows Explorer lives on in Windows 8, but with the new name of File Explorer. And true to its predecessor, File Explorer also lets you manage your Surface's files, folders, and storage areas. That makes the program particularly handy for moving files on and off your Surface.

To open File Explorer and begin browsing your Surface's files and storage areas, follow these steps:

1. **Open the Desktop app with a tap on its Start screen tile.**

2. **Tap the File Explorer icon (shown in the margin), found on the left end of the desktop's *taskbar* — that strip along the desktop's bottom edge.**

   File Explorer appears, shown in Figure 12-2, letting you manage the files on your Surface.

Tapping an item from a drop-down menu

When you try to tap on an item from a desktop window's drop-down menu, you rarely hit the desired option with your finger on the first try.

So, when you encounter a drop-down menu — or any scrolling menu, for that matter — aim and tap your finger anywhere on the list: But *don't* lift your finger.

Instead, slide your finger up or down the list. As your finger moves, Windows highlights different choices. When Windows highlights the choice you were originally aiming for, *lift* your finger.

That little trick ensures you make the correct choice, saving you from tapping repeatedly until you eventually land on your desired option.

Frequently accessed places

Currently viewed button

Ribbon menu

Ribbon menu tabs

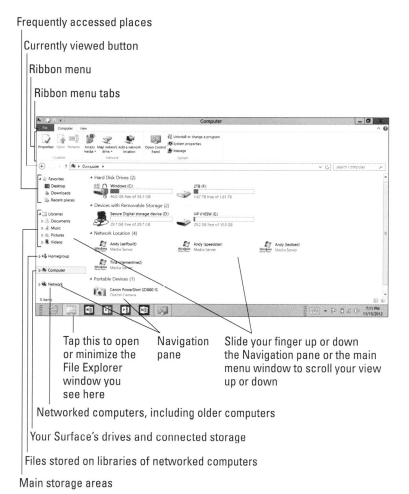

Tap this to open
or minimize the
File Explorer
window you
see here

Navigation
pane

Slide your finger up or down
the Navigation pane or the main
menu window to scroll your view
up or down

Networked computers, including older computers

Your Surface's drives and connected storage

Files stored on libraries of networked computers

Main storage areas

Figure 12-2: Tap Computer from File Explorer's left pane to see all your Surface's storage areas.

3. **To see your Surface's storage spaces and the files inside them, tap Computer from File Explorer's left pane, called the *Navigation pane.***

   There, you see all the drives accessible by your Surface: its internal hard drive, removable memory card, network locations, and anything you've plugged into its USB port, including flash drives, portable hard drives, and even digital cameras.

4. **To see inside a storage area, tap it on the Navigation pane.**

   Tap Libraries, for example, to see your Surface's main storage areas: Documents, Music, Pictures, and Videos. Tap Computer to see your Surface's memory card, flash drives, portable hard drives, or even to see photos stored on your camera. Tap any storage area you see, and File Explorer lists the files stored inside.

When you want to copy or move files or folders from one place to another, Windows makes you take two steps: First you *select* the items; second, you *copy* or *move* them to their new location.

The next section explains how to select items, be it files on a newly inserted flash drive or folders stored on a network. The section after that explains how to copy or move your selected items to a new destination on your Surface. (It also explains how to rename or delete selected files.)

Although desktop windows contain scroll bars, it's hard to position your fingertip inside those narrow bars. Instead, slide your finger up or down directly inside the Navigation pane; that scrolls the pane's contents up or down. The same applies to the items you see in the File Explorer window's left side.

Selecting files and folders with a fingertip

To select several items, hold down the Ctrl key on your Surface's keyboard while clicking items with the trackpad's mouse pointer or a mouse. Simple.

Selecting items or groups of items with your fingers, by contrast, can be one of a Surface's most maddening chores. It's fairly easy to select one item: just tap it, and Windows highlights it, showing that it's selected. But when you tap a second item, Windows selects *that* item, instead, deselecting the first.

How do you select more than *one* item just using your fingers? The key is a precisely placed tap under just the right conditions. The following steps show how to select items when you've detached your keyboard or folded it back to use your Surface as a tablet:

1. **Open File Explorer and navigate to the drive or folder containing the items you want to copy or move to or to your tablet.**

   Open File Explorer with a tap of its icon (shown in the margin) on the taskbar — that strip running along the desktop's bottom edge. When File Explorer appears, examine the Navigation pane along its left edge: It lists all of your Surface's storage areas.

Tap the storage area containing your items; that storage area's contents appear in File Explorer. Double-tap a flash drive, network location, or folder to open it. Keep digging until you've found the location of the item to be copied or moved.

2. **Switch to Details view.**

   File Explorer lets you view items in many different ways, and Details view makes it easiest to select things with your fingers. So, tap the View tab along the Ribbon menu's top edge, and then tap Details in the Layout section. File Explorer displays the items in Details view: rows of names of files and folders.

3. **To select a file, tap** *just to the left of a file's icon.* **A check box containing a check mark appears next to the file's icon.**

   This is the trickiest part. With the tip of your finger, tap just to the left of the file's or folder's name. When you tap in just the right spot, you place a check mark in the box that appears, shown in Figure 12-3.

As you quickly discover, this takes practice. If just one tap is off, Windows deselects *everything*, and selects only what you've just tapped. Keep trying, and you'll eventually find the sweet spot, just to the left of the icon.

After you select the items you want, move to the next section: Copying or Moving Files and Folders.

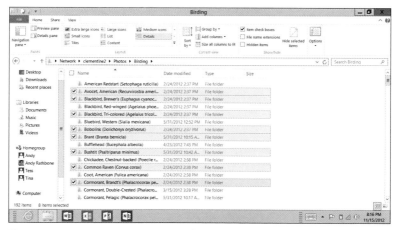

Figure 12-3: Tap just to the left of the file's or folder's icon, and a check mark appears, showing that you selected the file or folder.

✔ On the Start screen, a tap opens an item. On the desktop, by contrast, a tap *selects* an item. The desktop requires a *double-tap* — two quick taps in succession — to open an item.

✔ When selecting many items, it's sometimes easier to check the Select All check mark, and then tap to *deselect* unwanted items.

✔ To delete your selected items, tap the Ribbon menu's Home tab, and tap the Delete icon (shown in the margin).

✔ If you have a stylus for your Surface, it's often easier to select and deselect items by tapping their check boxes with the tip of a stylus.

✔ You can also *lasso* items using your finger or stylus: Draw a rectangle around your desired items, and Windows selects them for you.

✔ After fiddling around with your fingers on the desktop for a few minutes, you see why a mouse, trackpad, or stylus can be invaluable for precision desktop operations. If you didn't buy a Surface Touch or Type keyboard, I describe how to attach mice, both wired and Bluetooth, in Chapter 6.

Copying or moving files and folders

As you discovered in the previous section, selecting items with your fingers can be time-consuming. But after you've selected the items, it's easy to copy or move them to a new location by following these steps:

1. **From File Explorer, tap the Home tab near the top-left corner.**

   The Ribbon menu changes to show the icons seen in Figure 12-4.

2. **Tap the Move To or Copy to icons.**

   A menu drops down from your tapped icon, listing locations where you've previously saved items. If you spot your destination, tap it to complete the process.

   Don't spot the destination on the menu? Then choose the entry at the list's bottom: Choose Location.

   The Copy Items or Move Items window appears for you to choose your selected files destination.

Copy to

Move to | Delete

The Home tab | Rename

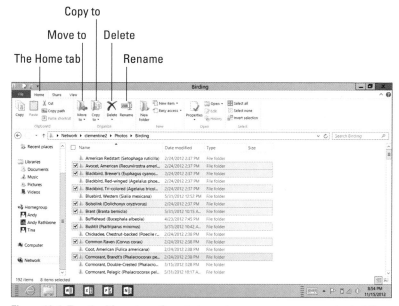

Figure 12-4: Tap the Move to or Copy to icons to move or copy your selected files.

3. **Select the items' destination from the window, and then tap the Copy or Move button to send your items to their new destination.**

   The Copy Items dialog box, shown in Figure 12-5, works much like a tiny Navigation pane that you see along the left edge of every folder. Tap Libraries to send your items to your Documents, Music, Pictures or Videos libraries, for example.

Figure 12-5: Tap a location and then tap the Copy or Move buttons to send your items to their final destination.

When a program *isn't* a program

Eager to promote its new Start screen system of computing, your Surface refers to its Start screen programs as "apps." However, your Surface also refers to *desktop programs* as apps. In the world of Windows 8, the word "program" no longer exists.

But because the entire computer industry will take some time to scrub the word "program" from its menus, software boxes, and websites, this book isn't scrubbing away the history of computing.

In this book, programs that run on the desktop are called *programs*. Programs that run on the Start screen are called *apps*.

Or, to send items to a flash drive, tap your flash drive from the drives listed in the window's Computer section.

When you've chosen your items' resting place, tap the Copy or Move button in the bottom of Figure 12-5. (The button's name depends on whether you tapped the Copy To or Move To icons in Step 2.)

 You can enlarge the Copy/Move dialog box by dragging its bottom-right corner outward. That brings more items into view.

Launching Desktop Programs

Although the Desktop app may seem like a self-contained world, it's not. The Desktop app tosses you back onto the Start screen on several occasions, most noticeably when you want to load a program.

Because the Windows 8 desktop lacks the Start button of yesteryear, you load a desktop program by following these steps:

1. **Return to the Start screen.**

   You can return to the Start screen by pressing your Surface's Windows button, pressing the Windows key on a keyboard, or swiping in from your Surface's right side and tapping the Windows icon on the Charms bar.

2. **Tap your desired program's icon from the Start screen.**

   I describe how to load programs from the Start screen in Chapter 4, but here are some quick tips:

   • If your desired program doesn't have a tile on the Start screen, swipe up from the bottom of your Surface's screen and tap the All Apps icon. The Start screen changes to show icons for *all* of your installed apps and programs.

• Desktop programs appear along the All Apps screen's farthest right edge.

When you tap the desktop program's icon, Windows 8 returns you to the Desktop app and begins running the program on the desktop.

Mastering Basic Window Mechanics

The key to maneuvering windows on the desktop with your finger is to think of your finger as a mouse pointer. Then follow these rules:

✔ To move a window around on the screen, use your finger to drag the window's title bar — that thick strip along its top edge. When you drag the window to its desired position, lift your finger, and the window stays in place.

✔ To make a window consume exactly half the screen, drag it with your finger all the way to the screen's right or left edge. As your finger reaches the edge, the window begins to resizes itself; lift your finger, and the window consumes exactly half the screen. This helps you position two windows side by side, handy when copying files from a flash drive to your Surface.

✔ To close a window, tap the X in its upper-right corner.

✔ To minimize a window, tap the little line icon near the window's upper-right corner.

✔ To maximize a window, tap the middle of the three icons shown in the window's upper-right corner.

✔ To shift your focus from one window to another, tap anywhere on the window you want to begin using.

Snapping an App Alongside the Desktop

Windows 8's Start screen and Desktop app live in very separate worlds. The Start screen is "modern," while the Desktop app is "traditional." They look and behave nothing alike, and, for the most part, they each work apart from each other.

TIP

Adding desktop programs to the taskbar

To skip some trips to the Start screen, add your favorite desktop programs to the desktop's *taskbar* — that strip along the desktop's bottom edge. To stock your taskbar with your favorite programs, follow these steps:

1. **From the Start screen, slide your finger up from the bottom edge to reveal the App bar, and then tap the All Apps icon.**

   The Start screen reveals icons for every app and program installed on your Surface.

2. **Select a favorite desktop program by sliding your finger up or down slightly on its icon.**

   A check mark appears next to the program's name, and the menu along the screen's bottom changes.

3. **From the bottom menu, tap the Pin to Taskbar icon.**

   The next time you visit the desktop, that program's icon is waiting on the task-bar, where you can launch it with a tap. By stocking the taskbar with your favorite programs, you can minimize your trips to the Start screen.

Sometimes, though, it's helpful to mix the two, perhaps placing your Calendar app next to your desktop to show your next appointment.

Windows 8 does that with a feat called *snapping* an app, and the result looks like Figure 12-6.

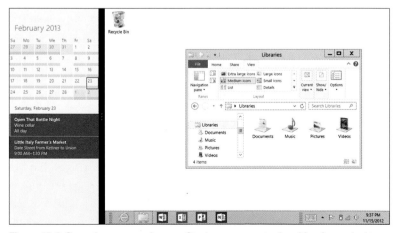

Figure 12-6: Snapping an app places a Start screen app to the side of your desktop.

Follow these steps to snap any Start screen app to the side of your desktop:

1. **Open the Desktop app, and then open any Start screen app.**

   To reach the Start screen from the desktop, press the Windows key at the bottom of your Surface's screen. Find the app you want to view alongside the desktop, and tap the app to bring it to the screen.

2. **Switch back to the desktop.**

   Slide your finger inward from the screen's left edge, dragging the desktop back onto the screen.

3. **Snap the app against your desktop.**

   This is the tricky part: *Slowly* drag your finger inward from the screen's left edge; your most recently opened app appears, following along with the motion of your finger. When you see a vertical strip appear onscreen, lift your finger; the app snaps itself to the screen's left edge.

When the app snaps against the desktop's left edge, a small vertical bar separates it from your desktop. The snapped app stays in place, even if you head back to the Start screen and run a few apps. When you return to the desktop, your snapped app remains stuck to the desktop's side.

App snapping works well for a few tasks, but it includes more rules than a rebate coupon:

- You can't snap an app to the side of the Start screen or any Smart screen apps. Apps can only snap to the side of your desktop.

- You can't snap an app onto each side of your desktop. You can only snap one app on one side.

- To unsnap the app, use your finger to drag that vertical bar back toward the screen's closest edge.

- Snapped apps are a fixed size; you can't make them slightly wider or narrower.

- Not all apps perform well when snapped. Some become so tiny they're nearly invisible.

- To unsnap a snapped app, drag the vertical line back to the screen's closest edge. When that vertical line reaches the edge, the snapped app unsnaps.

Chapter 13

Working in Microsoft Office

*I*t's no coincidence that the Surface with Windows RT includes a free, installed copy of Microsoft's Office Home and Student 2013 RT. Those popular programs — Word, PowerPoint, Excel, and OneNote — are all many people need.

Your Surface with Windows RT can read, save, and create Office files stored nearly anywhere: on your Surface, a flash drive, a networked PC, or on *SkyDrive*, the online storage place accessible by any PC.

These programs aren't pre-installed on the Surface with Windows 8 Pro, but if you install them, this chapter helps bring you up to speed on the basics on opening, saving, and printing Office files.

Opening, Saving, and Printing in Office 2013 RT

Microsoft's Office Home and Student 2013 RT includes three popular programs designed specifically to run on the Windows RT version of the Surface:

✔ **Word:** The industry-standard word processor, Word lets you create anything from letters to table-filled reports.

✔ **PowerPoint:** If you've sat through a corporate presentation shown on a projector or large TV, you've probably seen PowerPoint in action.

✔ **Excel:** A staple of accountants, Excel creates large tables for calculating complex formulas, handy for everything from household budgets to stock market projections.

Although the three programs do very different things, they all open, save, and print files in the same way.

This section walks you through each step of opening, saving, and printing files. I also explain how to save time by starting work with a free *template* — a pre-formatted document where you need only fill in the blanks.

 OneNote, a note-organizing program, works a little differently, so I give it a separate section at the chapter's end.

Opening a document

Whether you want to create a new document, open an existing one, or start working from a template, follow these steps to open a document in Word, Excel, or PowerPoint:

1. **From the Start screen, tap the tile of the program you want to open: Word, Excel, or PowerPoint.**

   If you don't spot your desired program on the Start screen, tap the Desktop app's tile. When the desktop appears, tap your desired program's icon from the desktop's *taskbar*, that strip along the bottom, and your chosen program fills the screen.

Taking the tour

Mixed in with other documents on the Open screen shown in Figure 13-1 is a tile called Take a Tour. By all means, tap the Take a Tour icon, even if you're familiar with the program. It offers a short guide and tips for how to put the program to work.

It's short, and it introduces some new features introduced in the version installed on your Surface with Windows RT: Office Home and Student 2013 RT, which Microsoft released in October, 2012. (It can still open your documents created in older versions of the program.)

---

2. **When your chosen program appears, tap what you'd like to open.**

Microsoft Word, for example, shown in Figure 13-1, shows how each program offers four ways of starting work:

* **Open a recently accessed document:** The Recent pane along the left edge lists your seven most-recently accessed documents. Tap a document's name, and it returns to the screen, ready for more work.

* **Start a new document:** Tap the Blank Document icon, and the program presents a blank page, ready for you to begin creating a new document from scratch.

* **Open a template:** Office's time-saving templates come pre-formatted, letting you concentrate on the content rather than the format or design. I give templates their own section later in this chapter.

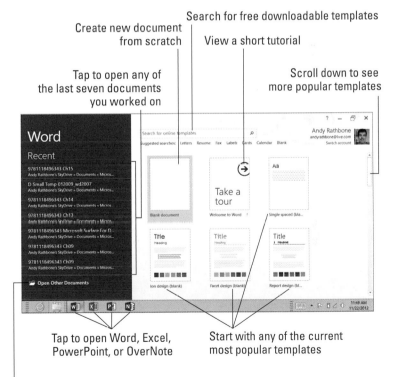

Figure 13-1: Choose among an existing document, a template, or creating a new document from scratch.

- **Search for a new template:** Hundreds of templates await online. Type **resume** into the Search box, for example, press the Enter key, and choose among dozens of pre-formatted resumes.

If you want to open a document not listed here, move to Step 3.

3. **Tap Open Other Documents, navigate to your existing document and load it with a tap of the Open button.**

Tap Open Other Documents from the bottom of the Recent pane, and the Open window appears, shown in Figure 13-2. The Open window lists your storage areas in the center column; to the right, it lists the currently selected storage area's most recently accessed folders and documents.

Previous page

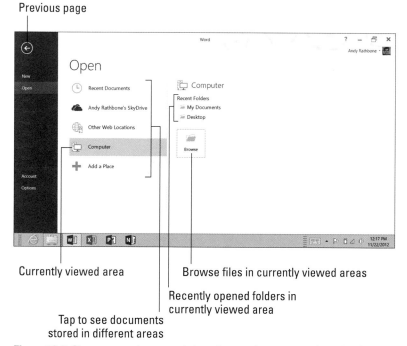

Currently viewed area

Browse files in currently viewed areas

Recently opened folders in currently viewed area

Tap to see documents stored in different areas

Figure 13-2: Choose your document's location, tap its name, and tap the Open button.

To open a listed document, tap its name. Still don't see it? Then tap one of the Open window's five main storage areas:

- **Recent Documents:** The opening screen shown earlier in Figure 13-1 only shows your past seven recently accessed documents. This area, however, shows the past two dozen documents you've opened. If you've opened the document before, chances are, it's listed here, waiting to be opened with a tap.

- **SkyDrive:** This lets you open files stored on SkyDrive, your online storage space covered in Chapter 6. By storing your files on SkyDrive, you can work on them either from your Surface or your desktop PC.

- **Other Web Locations:** Sometimes used by corporations, this lets you access folders stored on other websites.

- **Computer:** A popular choice, this shows recently accessed documents. It also offers a Browse button, where you can open files already stored on your Surface, or any stored on an attached flash drive or portable hard drive.

- **Add a Place:** Tap this shortcut to add other online storage places as Microsoft begins supporting them.

Tap the Browse button to navigate to documents inside a storage area, and then open your desired document with a tap on its name.

When you're having trouble finding a document, try any of these tips:

- When searching for a document you've worked on before, scan the Recent sections first. Tap likely suspects and take a peek. Guessed wrong? Close them with a tap in the program's upper-right corner and start again.

- Can't find a document *anywhere?* Then head back to the Start screen with a press of your Windows key. Begin typing a keyword contained in your wayward document and tap the word Files in the Search pane that appears on the right. Your Surface lists every file containing the word you typed.

- To find and edit a file stored on a newly inserted flash drive or portable hard drive, tap Computer in Step 3 and then tap the Browse button. When a miniature File Explorer window appears, tap your flash drive's letter in the Computer section of the Navigation pane along the miniature window's right edge.

- You can also open documents directly from File Explorer. If you spot your desired document on your recently inserted flash drive, double-tap its name: The program that created the document appears, with your document in tow.

The fine print

The version of Office Home and Student 2013 bundled with the Surface with Windows RT is the real thing: It's almost identical to the version of Office Home and Student 2013 sold in the stores for "normal" desktop computers. Microsoft explains the details of the differences at http://office.com/officeRT.

However, both versions of the program are licensed for *non-commercial* use only. To legally create documents for work, your business needs a volume licensing contract with Microsoft with commercial-use license coverage. Ask your business's IT person to see if you qualify, and what additional options are available.

Starting from a template

In days of old, we often started from scratch with a sheet of paper. Yet that paper could probably be called a *template*: the preformatted lines across the page gave us something to follow as we wrote.

Today's templates offer much more than simple lines. Microsoft offers thousands of free templates for creating elaborate resumes, reports, invitations, schedules, calendars, or even stock reports that automatically create themselves when you type in a stock symbol.

To start working from a template, follow these steps:

1. **From the Start screen, tap the tile of the program you want to open: Word, Excel, or PowerPoint.**

2. **When the program appears, tap the template you'd like to open, and then tap Create to open the template.**

    Figure 13-1, earlier in this chapter, lists just a few of the many free templates available, sorted by current popularity. During the holidays, you see more party invitations in Word, for example; in September, you see more templates for school activities.

    To see other popular templates in Excel, for example, scroll down the screen by dragging the scroll bar down the screen. Tap any template's icon for a quick preview, shown in Figure 13-3.

    If the current popular templates don't meet your needs, move to Step 3.

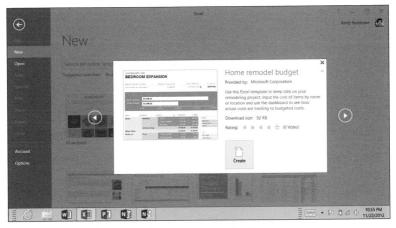

Figure 13-3: Tap a listed template to see more details.

3. **Search for an unlisted template by typing a keyword in the Search for Online Templates bar along the top and pressing Enter. When you see a template you want, tap the Create button to download the template and begin working.**

   Microsoft offers thousands of free templates online, searchable by key word. Type Expense into the Search bar (or tap the word Expense beneath the bar), for example, and Excel shows hundreds of expense-related templates shown in Figure 13-4.

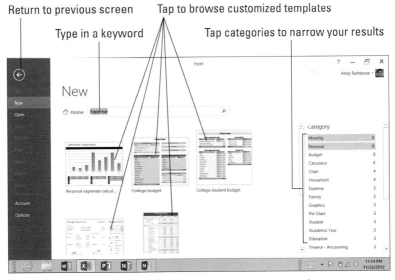

Figure 13-4: Tap a category to further narrow down your search.

Narrow down your themes by choosing from the categories, shown along the left of Figure 13-4. That figure, for example, shows expense-related templates in the categories of Monthly and Personal.

Tap a template to see a preview, as shown earlier in Figure 13-3; tap the Create button to download and open the template.

Word, Excel, and PowerPoint offer thousands of templates from a wide variety of categories. It's much faster to adapt a template to meet your needs rather than starting from scratch.

- ✔ To save space, Microsoft didn't bundle Office templates with your Surface. You must be connected to the Internet to download them.

- ✔ Before beginning a project, spend some time browsing and downloading potential templates. That way you can still work from a template when offline.

- ✔ To browse Microsoft's templates with Internet Explorer, visit `http://office.microsoft.com/en-us/templates`. Templates you download await you in your Downloads folder, available in the Navigation pane along the left edge of every folder.

Saving your work

As soon as you begin creating your document, *save it*. By saving it, you've done two things:

- ✔ You've created something to fall back on just in case you accidentally mess up your current work.

- ✔ You've created a starting point should you need to rush out the door and return later.

To save your work in Word, Excel, or PowerPoint, follow these steps:

1. **Tap the Save icon in the screen's top left corner.**

   The Save icon, which resembles a 25-year-old floppy disk, fetches the Save As window, shown in Figure 13-5.

2. **Choose a location for your document.**

   Two choices await you, depending on your plans for the document:

- **SkyDrive:** Choose this, your storage space on the Internet, if you plan on accessing the document from other computers. I describe SkyDrive in Chapter 6.

- **Computer:** If you plan on keeping the document on your Surface or e-mailing it to somebody, choose this option, and then select My Documents as your final destination. Every program and app can easily access files stored inside that folder.

3. **Choose a name for your Document and tap the Save button.**

   Your helpful program offers a generic name, like **Presentation1**, which certainly won't help you locate your work. Change the suggested name to something more descriptive that will help you remember the document next week.

Figure 13-5: Choose a name for your work and a place to save it.

Printing your document

After you've finished and saved your document, follow these steps to print your finished work in Word, Excel, or PowerPoint:

1. **Tap the word File from the Ribbon menu.**

   The Ribbon menu stretches across each program's top. Tapping different words on the Ribbon – *Format*, for example – shows different commands related to that formatting your document.

   Tapping File reveals *file*-related commands, shown in Figure 13-6, including Print.

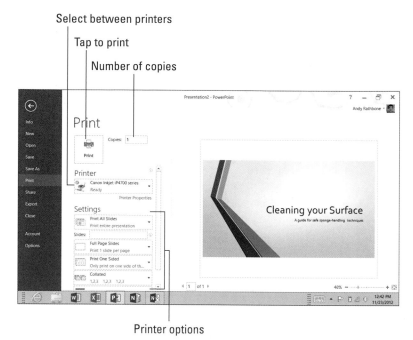

Figure 13-6: Choose Print from the left edge, choose your printing options, and tap the Print button at the top.

2. **Choose your printer and adjust its settings, if necessary, and tap Print.**

   If you only want one copy of your document sent to the printer you normally use, just tap the Print button.

   If you need to do a little tweaking, adjust the settings shown in Figure 13-6 before tapping the print button.

   ✔ Desktop programs include built-in print commands that allow more customized print jobs. Start screen apps, by contrast, require you to open the Charms bar, choose Devices, and select your printer in order to print.

   ✔ Need to give a PowerPoint presentation? I explain how to connect your Surface to a projector or external display in Chapter 6.

Taking Notes with OneNote

A computerized three-ring tabbed binder, Microsoft's OneNote organizes your notes. It's not picky, letting you add notes in *any* form: typed by hand, copied from websites, recorded as audio, captured as a photograph or video, or even handwritten with a stylus on the Surface's screen.

Students have embraced OneNote because it lets them open a Chemistry section, create a new tab for each new lecture or subject, and fill it with freeform notes, including photos of the blackboard or hand-written equations.

OneNote organizes your notes in three main ways:

- ✔ **Notebooks:** Everything starts with a notebook, which holds all of your notes. You can create as many notebooks as you wish, each designed around its own theme. OneNote starts with two notebooks: The Personal notebook contains notes dealing with you and your home; the Work notebook helps you track your work-related projects.

- ✔ **Categories:** Each notebook can have several categories to separate your projects. The Home notebook could have a Remodeling category, for example, as well as a Shopping List category.

- ✔ **Pages:** Here's where you break down your categories even further. The Home notebook's Recipe category could have a page for each recipe.

Follow these steps to create a new Notebook in OneNote, add new categories, and add pages to the categories:

1. **Open OneNote, tap File from the top menu and tap New.**

   To create a new notebook, begin by choosing a storage location, usually SkyDrive, so it can be accessed from any of your computers. Then type a name for your Notebook, in this case, Shopping List.

2. **Choose whether to share your notebook with others.**

   When the Microsoft OneNote window appears, you can tap the Invite People button to give others access to your OneNote file. That's handy when creating projects at work, for example, or creating a shopping list that can be on every family member's phone.

   To keep it private, tap the Not Now button; you can always share it later.

3. **Type notes into your project, adding Categories and Pages as needed.**

   OneNote appears, shown in Figure 13-7, letting you add Categories and pages to organize your notes. If you want, save time by starting from a template: Tap Insert from the top menu, choose Page Templates from the drop-down menu, and choose from the templates offered on the screen's right edge.

4. **To add a category tab, tap the plus sign to the right of the last tab and then type the category's name.**

   Figure 13-7 offers two categories, for example: one for 99 Ranch Supermarket, the other for a local health food store. Each category contains a shopping list for a different store.

   To change or delete a tabbed category, rest your finger on its tab until the pop-up menu appears, and then choose your option.

5. **To add a page to the currently viewed category, tap the words Add Page atop the right column and type in a page name.**

   For example, the 99 Ranch category lists some recipes for favorite dishes, making it easy to look over the ingredient list while at the store.

When you're through taking notes, simply stop and close the program with a tap on the X in its upper-right-hand corner. The program automatically saves your work with the name and location you chose in Step 1.

Microsoft offers OneNote for PCs, Apple computers, and every smart phone, letting access your notes from nearly any location.

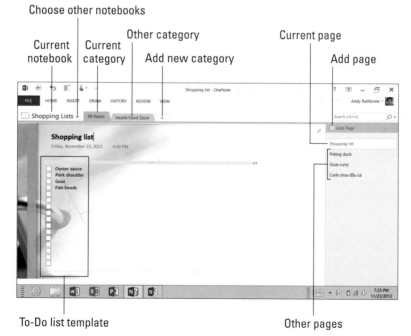

Figure 13-7: This Shopping List notebook shows two categories and three pages.

Chapter 14

Settings and Troubleshooting

. . . .

In This Chapter

▶ Customizing your Surface's settings

▶ Refreshing your Surface's operating system

▶ Resetting your Surface to factory condition

▶ Troubleshooting your Surface

▶ Sending in your Surface for repair

. . . .

*O*ccasionally, your Surface will misbehave. Sometimes it's just a minor irritation; other times, your Surface simply refuses to obey orders.

To keep your Surface running smoothly, this section explains how to tweak your Surface through its bundle of switches in the PC Settings area. I explain how to refresh your Surface when it's *really* misbehaving. And I show how to reset your Surface to factory condition when you're ready to start over.

And, if those things don't fix it, the last section explains how to contact Microsoft for repairing or replacing your Surface.

Customizing Your Surface through PC Settings

The Start screen's control panel, called the PC Settings screen, lets you polish off your Surface's rough edges. Each section in the PC Settings screen lets you customize a different area of your Surface's behavior.

To open the PC Settings Screen and begin tweaking your Surface to meet your needs, follow these steps:

1. **From any screen, slide your finger inward from the right edge to fetch the Charms bar and then tap the Settings icon.**

2. **When the Settings pane appears, tap the words Change PC Settings from the bottom edge.**

The PC Settings screen appears, shown in Figure 14-1. The pane on the left lists the categories of settings; tap a category, and that category's options spill out to the right.

Figure 14-1: The PC Settings screen lets you customize your Surface's behavior.

The rest of this section explains each category in PC Settings, and the settings most likely needing a bit of tweaking. The changes you make, usually by tapping a toggle switch, take place immediately.

Settings not found in this section, like Family Safety, and changing your Surface's name, can be found in the Desktop app's Control Panel. To find that, open the Desktop app, tap the Charms bar's Settings icon, and tap Control Panel from atop the Settings pane.

Personalize

The Personalize screen lets you change three areas: the lock screen that appears when you turn on or wake up your Surface, the Start screen's background colors and patterns, and your account photo.

Changing your sign-in account

You may want to change the account you use to sign in on your Surface. For example, you may want to sign on with the same account you use for your Xbox, or you may want to switch to a newly remembered Microsoft account.

The simplest solution is to create a new User Account for your new Microsoft account by following these steps:

1. **Open the Settings charm, and then tap Change PC settings.**

2. **Tap Add a User.**

   Type in the e-mail address associated with your newly remembered Windows Live ID (or the e-mail address associated with your Xbox gamer tag).

3. **Log back on to your old account and then move all of your data to your Surface's Public folders.**

   Double-click a library — Music, for example — and you see both the My Music folder and the Public library, where you should now copy all of your music.

Finally, log onto your new account and copy your files from the Public folders back into your own folders. When you're through, you can log off your old account and log onto your new account. After a few days, feel free to delete your old account, when you're sure you no longer need it. (Make sure you've elevated your new account to Administrator, so you're able to delete the old account.)

Deleting your old account also deletes anything you've purchased with it, including apps, movies, songs, and other items.

- ✔ **Lock screen:** Tap the words Lock Screen to see and change your current lock screen photo. Tap one of the existing images, or tap Browse to select your own photo from your Photo library. At the screen's bottom, choose which icons should display bits of information on the Lock screen.

- ✔ **Start screen:** This lets you merge 20 background patterns with 25 colors to create 500 different Start screen combinations.

- ✔ **Account picture:** To change your account photo, tap Camera and take a quick snapshot. Or, tap Browse to create an account photo from pictures in your Pictures library.

Users

This lets you upgrade your user account from a Local to Microsoft account, if desired. Head here to change your password, as well.

Chances are, though, you visit here most often to add a new user account to your Surface by tapping the section's Add a User button.

Newly added users will need to follow the walkthrough steps in Chapter 4 to download waiting updates, both from Windows Update and the Windows Store.

If you're adding a child, choose to Turn on Family Safety, if desired, so you may monitor their computer use.

Notifications

When one of your apps does something exciting, it sends you a *notification:* a little box in your screen's top-right corner that displays the reason for the excitement — a new instant message, for example, or an upcoming appointment.

Head to the Notifications section to choose which, if any, programs may send announcements, as well as whether they can make noises when doing so.

Search

The Charm bar's Search option lets you search for missing apps, lost files, or hard-to-find Settings. Beneath the Apps, Files, and Settings icons, you also see a list of searchable apps.

Tap the Search pane's Maps app, for example, type **Alaska**, and the Maps app pops up, ready to offer driving directions.

If you *don't* want an app listed as searchable within the Search pane, this area of PC Settings lets you toggle its removal.

Share

This rarely used setting lets you choose which apps appear on the Share pane's list of destinations. (To see the Share pane, open the Charms bar and tap Share.) For example, when Facebook graces Windows 8 with an app, you can add (or remove) Facebook in this section.

General

Although this section sounds the most boring, you just might spend most of your time here. Here are a few gems, as well as a few misleading items:

- ✔ **Touch keyboard:** The settings offered here apply only to the *onscreen* keyboard. Unfortunately, the settings don't apply to the Touch or Type keyboards covered in Chapter 5.

- ✔ **Screen:** The Surface normally adjusts the screen's brightness automatically, dimming the screen at night and brightening it when you step outside. But if the constant dimming/brightening drives you batty, tap the Adjust My Screen Brightness Automatically toggle to turn it off. You can still adjust the screen brightness manually by tapping the Screen icon in the Settings pane. Keeping the brightness low preserves battery life.

- ✔ **Language:** Bilingual Surface owners can tap this to head straight to the Language area of the Desktop app's Control Panel. There, you can choose from keyboard layouts popular in other countries.

- ✔ **Available storage:** If you're running out of storage space, tap this to see a list of apps, sorted with the largest ones at the top. Delete the biggest hogs to regain some space. (Apps can't be stored on your memory card, unfortunately.)

I cover this section's last three options, *Refresh*, *Remove Everything*, and *Advanced Startup*, in this chapter's Troubleshooting section.

Privacy

This bone tossed in for privacy advocates lets you choose whether apps can use your general location (handy with maps and weather), and your name and account picture (used by many social networks).

A third option lets Microsoft receive lists of websites used by apps, hopefully so Microsoft can weed out apps doing unscrupulous things.

Devices

This handy list shows all the devices now- or once-attached to your Surface. Unfortunately, it doesn't let you do anything but remove them by tapping the minus sign to the right of their name.

The gem here is Add a Device, listed at the top. Tap that to add Bluetooth gadgets like mice, keyboards, and headsets, as described in Chapter 6.

Wireless

Only three toggle switches live here, but they're all handy. Tap the Airplane Mode toggle to turn off your Wi-Fi before heading onto a plane. The other two toggles control Wi-Fi and Bluetooth. Feel free to turn off Bluetooth to extend your battery life if you never connect with Bluetooth gadgets like wireless mice and keyboards.

Ease of Access

These switches help adapt the Surface to people with physical challenges. The High Contrast switch, for example, helps the vision-impaired by reducing all distraction. And Windows' Narrator, a Windows chestnut for years, reads menus and text with its robotic tone.

Sync Your Settings

Microsoft kindly remembers the settings of Microsoft account owners. Log onto another PC with your Microsoft account, and your settings, passwords, app purchases, favorite websites, and more, ride along, making that other PC behave much like your own.

This section lets you choose which settings, if any, you *don't* want to travel with you. (For example, if you prefer your Surface's wallpaper to be different than that on your Windows 8 desktop PC, tap the Personalize toggle to Off.)

Homegroup

The Surface with Windows RT can't *start* a homegroup, but it can join an existing one. The Surface with Windows 8 Pro, by contrast, can both start and join an existing homegroup. This section lists the password of the homegroup you've joined, if any.

Windows Update

Your Surface is very new, and updates arrive frequently to fix problems and smooth out rough spots. You can tap Check Updates here to find the latest. For more information about Windows Update, flip back to Chapter 3.

Troubleshooting

Occasionally, your Surface either misbehaves or falls ill. This section covers possible treatment plans, as well as a few tweaks to solve specific problems.

Fixing problem apps

When an app doesn't seem to be working correctly anymore, follow these steps to uninstall it, and then reinstall it from the Windows Store. (This works for both free and paid apps; the store remembers your purchase and lets you download the app again without paying twice.)

1. **From the Start screen, select your problem app's tile or icon.**

   To select an app, drag it down slightly with your finger. A check mark appears by the app, and the App bar appears along the screen's bottom edge.

2. **Tap the Uninstall icon on the App bar.**

   Your Surface uninstalls the app.

3. **Visit the Windows Store and reinstall the app.**

   From the Windows Store, slide your down finger slightly from the screen's top, and then tap the words Your Apps that appear along the screen's top edge. Tap the name of your formerly misbehaving app, and then tap the Install button from the App bar along screen's bottom edge.

Your app reinstalls itself onto your Start screen's farthest right edge. Hopefully, your app has enjoyed its vacation and returned in a better mood.

Backing up your Surface

Your Surface does a remarkable job of backing up itself. Your Microsoft account remembers how you personalize your Surface, as well as the settings you change. It also remembers your e-mail accounts, calendar information, contacts, favorite websites, and even many of your passwords.

The Windows Store remembers the apps you've installed and purchased, making it easy to download them again. Any files you store on SkyDrive are backed up there.

That leaves the files you've stored in your Windows libraries. You can back those up on your Surface's memory card or a portable hard drive with Windows 8's File History program by following these steps:

1. **Insert your memory card or plug a portable hard drive into the USB port.**

   I describe how to do both in Chapter 6, if you want more information.

2. **Tap the pop-up notification that says Tap to Choose What Happens with Removable Drives.**

   Don't see the pop-up notification? Then unplug your drive or remove your memory card and wait a few seconds. Then reinsert it, watching so you can tap the notification.

   When you tap the notification, a second window appears, offering several options.

3. **Select the Configure This Drive for Backup option. Then, when the File History window appears, tap the Turn On button.**

   Put your drive in a safe place, and remember to reconnect it often, so your Surface can create another, more recent backup.

   To view your backups, open the Desktop app, tap the Charms bar's Settings icon, and tap Control Panel from the top of the Settings pane.

   When the Control Panel appears, open the System and Security section and tap File History. There, you see options for turning File History on and off, as well as a link on the left that says Restore Personal Files.

   I explain more about File History in my larger book, *Windows 8 For Dummies*, published by John Wiley & Sons, Inc.

Refreshing your Surface

When your Surface isn't working correctly, you can tell it to reinstall its operating system, but save your files. It's a quick fix, as you can easily reinstall your apps from the Windows Store. But it poses a problem for owners of the Windows 8 Pro version.

On the Windows 8 Pro version of the Surface, the Refresh feature also removes all of the *programs* you've installed on your Desktop app. Before using the Refresh feature, make sure you have your program's original installation discs handy because you need to reinstall them all.

To Refresh your Surface, follow these steps:

1. **Swipe in from the right edge of the screen, tap Settings, and then tap Change PC settings.**

2. **Tap the General section.**

3. **In the Refresh Your PC Without Affecting Your Files section, tap the Get Started button.**

4. **When your Surface wakes up, you're left with a few tasks:**

   • Visit the PC Settings screen's Windows Update section and download any waiting updates.

   • Open the Windows Store app and reinstall your apps.

   • On the Surface with Windows 8 Pro, open the Windows desktop. There, you find a waiting list of your uninstalled desktop programs, along with links to where you can download and reinstall most of them.

Refreshing your Surface takes much less time on a Windows RT version because you needn't worry about reinstalling desktop programs. (The Office programs will still be there, although you need to update them again with Windows Update.) But on a Surface with Windows 8 Pro, tracking down and reinstalling all those desktop programs can be a nightmare.

Resetting your Surface

This last-resort option wipes your Surface completely clean, removing *everything*. When it wakes back up, it behaves like it was just removed from its shiny new box. It's a drastic measure, but it's one that always works when your Surface seems beyond repair.

I can't even sign in!

If your Surface won't even reach the Sign On screen, you're not without hope. You can troubleshoot, refresh, or reset your Surface to factory conditions by following these steps:

1. **With your Surface turned off, attach any type of keyboard. (A desktop keyboard plugged into your USB port will do, if you don't have a Touch or Type keyboard cover.)**

2. **Turn on your Surface by pressing its power button.**

3. **At the Sign On screen, press and hold the Left Shift key.**

4. **Tap the Power icon in the screen's bottom-right corner, and tap Restart from the pop-up menu.**

   A light-blue screen appears on your Surface offering several options, including Troubleshoot.

5. **Tap Troubleshoot.**

   The Troubleshoot screen lets you Refresh or Reset your Surface. But before trying those, tap Advanced Options and then tap Automatic Repair.

If your Surface can't repair itself, follow these steps again, but choose Refresh or Repair in Step 5.

In Step 5, owners of the Windows RT version find a way to boot from their USB Recovery Drive, which I describe how to make in Chapter 3. Surface with Windows 8 Pro owners see an option to load a System Image backup.

 Resetting your Surface is also a good way to restore your Surface to factory conditions before giving it away, either to friends or charity.

 Resetting your Surface deletes *all* of your personal files, apps, desktop programs, and settings.

To reset your Surface to factory conditions, follow these steps:

1. **Swipe in from the right edge of the screen, tap Settings, and then tap Change PC settings.**

2. **Tap the General category.**

3. **In the section called Remove Everything and Reinstall Windows, tap Get Started, tap Next, and follow the instructions.**

When your Surface returns to life, page back to Chapter 3. Your Surface behaves just as it did when you first turned it on, and you need to choose a language and begin installing updates.

Servicing Your Surface through Microsoft

If your Surface includes problems you can't fix alone, drop by Microsoft's website at this address:

```
https://myservice.surface.com
```

After you enter your Microsoft account, the website walks you through registering your Surface, reporting problems, checking the status of service orders, checking your warranty status, replacing accessories, and, if desired, buying a service plan.

To find your Surface's serial number, flip open its kickstand; it's printed below the word *Surface*. The serial number for your Touch or Type keyboards is printed on the right side of the keyboard's spine. (You need to detach the keyboard from your Surface to see it.)

Chapter 15

Ten Essential Tips 'n' Tricks

A For Dummies book isn't the same without a Part of Tens chapter. With the Surface, the hard part is limiting it to just ten. After paring down the list from 20, here are 10 essential tips and tricks to wring the most out of your Surface.

When Lost, Swipe in from the Screen's Left Edge

Whenever you tap a link or another program on your Surface, the new item fills the screen, pulling you in deeply. When you finally close the app, the Start screen jumps in to fill the void.

But what were you working on *before* you went off track by tapping the link?

To find out, swipe in from the screen's left side. Your original app fills the screen, bringing you full circle to where you were before the distraction.

Search for Items by Typing Directly on the Start Screen

When you're searching for something, start typing its name directly onto the Start screen. Windows clears the screen and begins listing matches.

For example, type **camera** directly into the Start screen.

As you type the first letter, the Start screen switches to Search mode, listing every app containing the letter "c." As you keep typing, the list narrows, eventually showing only camera-related apps.

The Search pane clings to the screen's right edge, letting you direct your search away from apps and into other areas:

- ✓ **Settings:** Tap Settings from the Search pane, and your Surface lists camera-related settings.

- ✓ **Files:** To see any *files* containing the term camera, tap Files; the screen shows any of your files mentioning the word *camera*.

- ✓ **Specific apps:** Beneath the list of Apps, Files, and Settings, the Search pane lists specific apps. Tap one of those — Netflix, for example — to search for movies relating to the word *camera*.

Select Start Screen Tiles

Some items seem difficult to select, a precursor to deleting, moving, renaming, copying, or any other host of tasks. For example, a tap on a Start screen tile opens it rather than selects it. Holding down a finger on the tile doesn't fetch a menu. Perplexed finger jabs just scroll the item back and forth.

The trick to selecting difficult items like Start screen tiles is to slide your finger across them in the *opposite* direction that they scroll.

Start screen tiles normally slide from right to left. So, select them by sliding your finger *up or down* across the tile. This works when selecting photos, e-mails in the Mail app, and many other seemingly difficult-to-select items.

Take Screenshots

To take a snapshot of what you're seeing on the screen, hold down the Windows key below your Surface's screen and press the Down Volume toggle. The screen dims, and a screenshot appears in your Pictures library's Screenshots folder.

Stop the Screen from Rotating

Most of the time, you want the screen to rotate as you hold your Surface. That way, the screen's always right side up. Occasionally, though, you don't want it to rotate — perhaps you're reading a book or browsing websites.

 To keep the screen from rotating, open the Charms menu and tap on Settings. When the Settings pane appears, tap on the screen icon near bottom right (shown in the margin).

When the brightness bar appears, look at the Rotation Lock icon atop the bar; tap that icon to toggle autorotation on and off.

Note: The rotation lock automatically turns on when your Touch or Type keyboard is attached and folded out for use; it turns off when you fold the keyboard back (or detach it) to use your Surface as a tablet.

Tweak Your App's Settings

Every app offers a way to fine-tune its behavior through the Charms bar's Settings area. When something about an app irks you, see if you can change it: Fetch the Charms bar by sliding your finger in from the screen's right edge and tapping Settings. If an app can be changed, the Settings pane offers a way.

Keep Your Apps Up to Date

Windows 8's app ecosystem is new, and many publishers release updated versions of their apps on a regular basis. To find and install updates for your apps, keep an eye on the Start screen's Store app.

When apps are available, a small number appears in the Store's lower-right corner. Spot a number? Tap the Store app to find and install waiting updates.

Make a Recovery Drive

 I tossed this in as a sidebar in Chapter 3, but it's really not very difficult. If you have an old flash drive of at least 4 GB, dedicate it as a Recovery Drive for your Surface RT. If your Surface won't start someday, that Recovery Drive just might be the only thing to bring it back to life.

Use the Charms Bar for Apps

It's easy to open an app and then begin searching its menus for basic things like search, print, or even a way to adjust settings.

Yet, they're all there, and you've used them before: The Charms bar works not only on the Start screen, but on all the apps you buy in the Windows Store.

Looking for a movie in the Netflix app, for example? Fetch the Charms bar, and tap Search, and enter your sought-after film in the Search pane.

And if you need to print, open the Charms bar, tap Devices, and choose your printer from the Devices pane. (Not all apps can print, unfortunately.)

Be Patient

Microsoft deliberately left out many features from Windows 8, hoping that developers would step up and begin filling in all the holes. The Windows Store grows every day. If your sought-after app isn't there yet, give it a little time.

Index

Apple & Macs

iPad For Dummies
978-0-470-58027-1

iPhone For Dummies,
4th Edition
978-0-470-87870-5

MacBook For
Dummies, 3rd Edition
978-0-470-76918-8

Mac OS X Snow
Leopard For
Dummies
978-0-470-43543-4

Business

Bookkeeping For
Dummies
978-0-7645-9848-7

Job Interviews
For Dummies,
3rd Edition
978-0-470-17748-8

Resumes For
Dummies,
5th Edition
978-0-470-08037-5

Starting an
Online Business
For Dummies,
6th Edition
978-0-470-60210-2

Stock Investing
For Dummies,
3rd Edition
978-0-470-40114-9

Successful
Time Management
For Dummies
978-0-470-29034-7

Computer Hardware

BlackBerry
For Dummies,
4th Edition
978-0-470-60700-8

Computers For
Seniors
For Dummies,
2nd Edition
978-0-470-53483-0

PCs For Dummies,
Windows 7 Edition
978-0-470-46542-4

Laptops For
Dummies,
4th Edition
978-0-470-57829-2

Cooking & Entertaining

Cooking Basics
For Dummies,
3rd Edition
978-0-7645-7206-7

Wine For Dummies,
4th Edition
978-0-470-04579-4

Diet & Nutrition

Dieting For Dummies,
2nd Edition
978-0-7645-4149-0

Nutrition For
Dummies,
4th Edition
978-0-471-79868-2

Weight Training
For Dummies,
3rd Edition
978-0-471-76845-6

Digital Photography

Digital SLR Cameras
& Photography For
Dummies, 3rd Edition
978-0-470-46606-3

Photoshop Elements 8
For Dummies
978-0-470-52967-6

Gardening

Gardening Basics
For Dummies
978-0-470-03749-2

Organic Gardening
For Dummies,
2nd Edition
978-0-470-43067-5

Green/Sustainable

Raising Chickens
For Dummies
978-0-470-46544-8

Green Cleaning
For Dummies
978-0-470-39106-8

Health

Diabetes For
Dummies,
3rd Edition
978-0-470-27086-8

Food Allergies
For Dummies
978-0-470-09584-3

Living Gluten-Free
For Dummies,
2nd Edition
978-0-470-58589-4

Hobbies/General

Chess For Dummies,
2nd Edition
978-0-7645-8404-6

Drawing
Cartoons & Comics
For Dummies
978-0-470-42683-8

Knitting For Dummies,
2nd Edition
978-0-470-28747-7

Organizing
For Dummies
978-0-7645-5300-4

Su Doku For
Dummies
978-0-470-01892-7

Home Improvement

Home Maintenance
For Dummies,
2nd Edition
978-0-470-43063-7

Home Theater
For Dummies,
3rd Edition
978-0-470-41189-6

Living the
Country Lifestyle
All-in-One
For Dummies
978-0-470-43061-3

Solar Power Your
Home
For Dummies,
2nd Edition
978-0-470-59678-4

Internet

Blogging For
Dummies,
3rd Edition
978-0-470-61996-4

eBay For Dummies,
6th Edition
978-0-470-49741-8

Facebook For
Dummies, 3rd Edition
978-0-470-87804-0

Web Marketing
For Dummies,
2nd Edition
978-0-470-37181-7

WordPress
For Dummies,
3rd Edition
978-0-470-59274-8

Language & Foreign Language

French For Dummies
978-0-7645-5193-2

Italian Phrases
For Dummies
978-0-7645-7203-6

Spanish For
Dummies, 2nd Edition
978-0-470-87855-2

Spanish For
Dummies, Audio Set
978-0-470-09585-0

Math & Science

Algebra I
For Dummies,
2nd Edition
978-0-470-55964-2

Biology
For Dummies,
2nd Edition
978-0-470-59875-7

Calculus For
Dummies
978-0-7645-2498-1

Chemistry For
Dummies
978-0-7645-5430-8

Microsoft Office

Excel 2010 For
Dummies
978-0-470-48953-6

Office 2010 All-in-One
For Dummies
978-0-470-49748-7

Office 2010 For
Dummies,
Book + DVD Bundle
978-0-470-62698-6

Word 2010 For
Dummies
978-0-470-48772-3

Music

Guitar For Dummies,
2nd Edition
978-0-7645-9904-0

iPod & iTunes
For Dummies,
8th Edition
978-0-470-87871-2

Piano Exercises
For Dummies
978-0-470-38765-8

Parenting & Education

Parenting For
Dummies,
2nd Edition
978-0-7645-5418-6

Type 1 Diabetes
For Dummies
978-0-470-17811-9

Pets

Cats For Dummies,
2nd Edition
978-0-7645-5275-5

Dog Training
For Dummies,
3rd Edition
978-0-470-60029-0

Puppies For
Dummies,
2nd Edition
978-0-470-03717-1

Religion & Inspiration

The Bible For
Dummies
978-0-7645-5296-0

Catholicism For
Dummies
978-0-7645-5391-2

Women in the Bible
For Dummies
978-0-7645-8475-6

Self-Help & Relationship

Anger Management
For Dummies
978-0-470-03715-7

Overcoming Anxiety
For Dummies,
2nd Edition
978-0-470-57441-6

Sports

Baseball
For Dummies,
3rd Edition
978-0-7645-7537-2

Basketball
For Dummies,
2nd Edition
978-0-7645-5248-9

Golf For Dummies,
3rd Edition
978-0-471-76871-5

Web Development

Web Design
All-in-One
For Dummies
978-0-470-41796-6

Web Sites
Do-It-Yourself
For Dummies,
2nd Edition
978-0-470-56520-9

Windows 7

Windows 7
For Dummies
978-0-470-49743-2

Windows 7
For Dummies,
Book + DVD Bundle
978-0-470-52398-8

Windows 7 All-in-One
For Dummies
978-0-470-48763-1

Available wherever books are sold. For more information or to order direct: U.S. customers visit www.dummies.com or call 1-877-762-2974. U.K. customers visit www.wileyeurope.com or call (0) 1243 843291. Canadian customers visit www.wiley.ca or call 1-800-567-4797.